CLASSROOM
ASSESSMENT
SCORING
SYSTEM®

MANUAL K–3

CLASSROOM ASSESSMENT SCORING SYSTEM®

MANUAL K–3

by

Robert C. Pianta, Ph.D.
Center for Advanced Study in Teaching and Learning (CASTL)
University of Virginia, Charlottesville

Karen M. La Paro, Ph.D.
Department of Human Development and Family Studies
University of North Carolina at Greensboro

and

Bridget K. Hamre, Ph.D.
Center for Advanced Study in Teaching and Learning (CASTL)
University of Virginia, Charlottesville

PAUL·H·
BROOKES
PUBLISHING CO.®

Baltimore • London • Sydney

Paul H. Brookes Publishing Co.
Post Office Box 10624
Baltimore, Maryland 21285-0624

www.brookespublishing.com

Typeset by Barton Matheson Willse & Worthington, Baltimore, Maryland.
Classroom Assessment Scoring System®, K–3, is manufactured in the United States
of America by Versa Press, Inc., East Peoria, Illinois.
Classroom Assessment Scoring System®, Dimensions Overview, is manufactured in
the United States of America by H & N Printing & Graphics, Inc., Timonium, Maryland.

The *Classroom Assessment Scoring System®, Dimensions Overview,* accompanies
the *Classroom Assessment Scoring System® (CLASS®) Manual, K–3.* The *Classroom
Assessment Scoring System® (CLASS®) Form, Pre-K–3,* is intended for one-time
use only and can be purchased in packages of 10 (ISBN-13: 978-1-55766-943-8).
The *Classroom Assessment Scoring System® (CLASS®) Manual, Infant* (ISBN-13:
978-1-59857-604-7), *Toddler* (ISBN-13: 978-1-59857-259-9), and *Pre-K* (ISBN-13:
978-1-55766-941-4) are also available for purchase. To order, contact Brookes
Publishing Co., 1-800-638-3775; http://www.brookespublishing.com.

Fifth printing, April 2016.

Library of Congress Cataloging-in-Publication Data

Pianta, Robert C.
    Classroom assessment scoring system® (CLASS®) manual, k–3 / by Robert C.
Pianta, Karen M. La Paro, and Bridget K. Hamre.
        p.   cm.
    Includes bibliographical references and index.
    ISBN-13: 978-1-55766-942-1
    ISBN-10: 1-55766-942-2
    1. Education, Primary—United States—Evaluation.   2. Kindergarten—United
States—Evaluation.   3. Teacher–student relationships—United States—Evaluation.
I. La Paro, Karen M.   II. Hamre, Bridget K.   III. Title.

LB1511.P524 2008
372.1102'3—dc22   2007027235

British Library Cataloguing in Publication data are available from the British Library.

Contents

About the Authors

Robert C. Pianta, Ph.D., is Dean of the Curry School of Education, Director of the Center for Advanced Study in Teaching and Learning (CASTL), and Novartis U.S. Foudantion Professor of Education at the University of Virginia, Charlottesville. A former special education teacher, Dr. Pianta is a developmental, school, and clinical child psychologist whose work focuses on how children's experiences at home and in school affect their development. He is particularly interested in how relationships with teachers and parents as well as classroom experiences can help improve outcomes for at-risk children and youth. Dr. Pianta is a principal investigator on several major grants including MyTeachingPartner, the IES Interdisciplinary Doctoral Training Program in Risk and Prevention, and the National Institute of Child Health and Human Development (NICHD) Study of Early Child Care and Youth Development (SECCYD); a senior investigator with the National Center for Early Development and Learning (NCEDL); and Editor of the *Journal of School Psychology*. He is the author of more than 200 journal articles, chapters, and books in the areas of early childhood development, transition to school, school readiness, and parent–child and teacher–child relationships, and he consults regularly with federal agencies, foundations, and universities.

Karen M. La Paro, Ph.D., is an assistant professor with the University of North Carolina at Greensboro. She worked with inclusion projects and Head Start in Louisiana and received her doctoral degree in early childhood special education from the University of New Orleans. She has been research faculty working with the NICHD Study of Early Child Care as well as the NCEDL at the University of Virginia, Charlottesville. Her current research interests relate to issues of quality for early childhood classrooms focusing on studies of teacher–child interactions and professional development for teachers of young children.

Bridget K. Hamre, Ph.D., is Senior Scientist and Associate Director of CASTL at the University of Virginia, Charlottesville. After spending a few years as a first-grade teacher in Berkeley, California, she received her doctoral degree in clinical and school psychology from the University of Virginia. She works on a variety of projects related to understanding the components of teachers' interactions with students that promote positive academic and social development. This work includes consulting with teachers as a part of the innovative professional development intervention study, MyTeachingPartner. Dr. Hamre also is interested in educational policy, an interest that was fostered during her 2 years at Policy Analysis for California Education (PACE) at the University of California, Berkeley.

Contributors

Andrew J. Mashburn, Ph.D.
Senior Research Scientist
Center for Advanced Study of Teaching and Learning (CASTL)
University of Virginia
350 Old Ivy Way, Suite 100
Charlottesville, VA 22903

Jennifer Locasale-Crouch, Ph.D.
Research Faculty
Center for Advanced Study of Teaching and Learning (CASTL)
University of Virginia
350 Old Ivy Way, Suite 100
Charlottesville, VA 22903

Acknowledgments

We acknowledge the Foundation for Child Development (FCD) for its financial support in the development of the Classroom Assessment Scoring System® (CLASS®). The CLASS Pre-K and K–3 observation materials were developed in part with a grant from the FCD. These materials also were initially developed and field tested as part of classroom observation research conducted by the National Center for Early Development and Learning (NCEDL), with the support of a grant from the U.S. Department of Education. We express our appreciation for the input and expertise of our numerous NCEDL colleagues, including Don Bailey, Dick Clifford, Peg Burchinal, Carollee Howes, Donna Bryant, Diane Early, Sharon Ritchie, Gisele Crawford, and Marcia Kraft-Sayre.

The development of CLASS also was supported by the child care and classroom observation research conducted as part of the National Institute of Child Health and Human Development (NICHD) Study of Early Child Care and Youth Development (SECCYD). We appreciate the work of Laura Justice and her colleagues, who were instrumental in the addition to the Language Modeling dimension of CLASS. We could not have completed this project without the tireless work of Megan Stuhlman and Jason Downer, who spent many hours piloting, coding, and training people on CLASS. Throughout the project, numerous graduate students and staff have contributed their effort and time.

Finally, we thank the many teachers who welcomed us and allowed us to videotape in their classrooms. Their dedication to improved practice is an example of their professionalism and care for students.

Introduction

CHAPTER ONE

The Classroom Assessment Scoring System® (CLASS®) is an observation instrument developed to assess classroom quality in preschool through third-grade classrooms. This K–3 manual provides information on the theoretical and empirical foundations of the CLASS, an overview of the procedures for using the CLASS, and detailed descriptions and examples for each dimension as observed in kindergarten through third-grade classrooms.[1]

THEORETICAL AND EMPIRICAL FOUNDATIONS OF THE CLASS

The CLASS dimensions are based on developmental theory and research suggesting that interactions between students and adults are the primary mechanism of student development and learning (Greenberg, Domitrovich, & Bumbarger, 2001; Hamre & Pianta, 2007; Morrison & Connor, 2002; Pianta, 2006; Rutter & Maughan, 2002). The CLASS dimensions are based solely on interactions between teachers and students in classrooms; this system does not evaluate the presence of materials, the physical environment or safety, or the adoption of a specific curriculum. This distinction between *observed interactions* and physical materials or reported use of curriculum is important because in most early elementary settings, materials and curriculum are prevalent and fairly well-organized. The CLASS focuses on interactions between teachers and students and what teachers *do* with the materials they have.

The CLASS was developed based on an extensive literature review as well as on scales used in large-scale classroom observation studies in the National Institute of Child Health and Human Development (NICHD) Study of Early Care (NICHD Early Child Care Research Network [ECCRN], 2002; Pianta, La Paro, Payne, Cox, & Bradley, 2002) and the National Center for Early Development and Learning (NCEDL) MultiState Pre-K Study (Early et al., 2005). The dimensions assessed by the CLASS were derived from a review of constructs assessed in classroom observation instruments used in child care and elementary school research, literature on effective teaching practices, focus groups, and extensive piloting. The CLASS was designed to create a common metric and vocabulary that could be used to describe various aspects of quality across the early childhood and elementary grades.

---

[1]A preschool version also is available. The major dimensions remain the same between the preschool and K–3 versions; however the preschool version provides examples specific to classrooms with younger students.

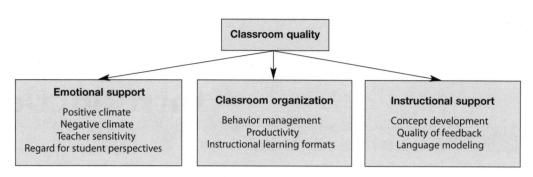

Figure 1.1. Overview of CLASS domains and dimensions.

It is significant to note that the domains and dimensions used by the CLASS to define and assess classroom quality are common across the preschool to third-grade period. However, the ways these dimensions are manifested are specific to particular developmental levels or age groups (i.e., preschool versus grades K–3). In other words, an underlying assumption of the CLASS is that there is *heterotypic continuity* in quality teaching across grade levels: The same underlying dimensions comprise high-quality classrooms throughout this age range; however, the ways that these dimensions are demonstrated in classroom practice may shift as children mature. By providing a common metric and language for discussion of quality *across grades*, the CLASS addresses problems with grade-to-grade transition and the need for coherence (Bogard & Takanishi, 2005) while providing a context-specific and developmentally sensitive metric for each grade level.

At the broadest level, interactions between teachers and students can be grouped into three domains: Emotional Support, Classroom Organization, and Instructional Support. Figure 1.1 provides an overview of these domains and the dimensions within each domain as measured by the CLASS. This organizational structure for classroom interactions has been validated in more than 3,000 classrooms from preschool to fifth grade (Hamre, Mashburn, Pianta, & Downer, 2006).

CLASS DOMAINS

The following discussion elaborates on the major domains of classroom experience assessed by the CLASS. A more complete discussion of the theoretical and empirical basis for the CLASS is available elsewhere (Hamre & Pianta, 2007; La Paro, Pianta, & Stuhlman, 2004).

Emotional Support

Children's social and emotional functioning in the classroom is increasingly recognized as an indicator of school readiness (Blair, 2002; Denham & Weissberg, 2004; Raver, 2004), a potential target for intervention (Greenberg, Weissberg, & O'Brien, 2003; Zins, Bloodworth, Weissberg, & Walberg, 2004), and even a student outcome that might be governed by a set of standards similar to those for academic achievement (Illinois State Board of Education, 2004). Children who are motivated and connected to others in the early years of schooling are much more likely to establish positive trajectories of development in both social and academic domains (Hamre & Pianta, 2001; Ladd, Birch, & Buhs, 1999; Pianta, Steinberg, & Rollins, 1995; Silver, Measelle, Essex, & Armstrong, 2005). Teachers' abilities to support social and emotional functioning in the classroom are therefore central to any conceptualization of effective classroom practice. The dimensions included in the Emotional Support domain on the CLASS include the following:

- Positive Climate: The emotional connection, respect, and enjoyment demonstrated between teachers and students and among students

- Negative Climate: The level of expressed negativity such as anger, hostility, or aggression exhibited by teachers and/or students in the classroom

- Teacher Sensitivity: Teachers' awareness of and responsivity to students' academic and emotional concerns

- Regard for Student Perspectives: The degree to which teachers' interactions with students and classroom activities place an emphasis on students' interests, motivations, and points of view

These dimensions collectively and separately predict to students' performance on standardized tests of literacy skills in preschool and first grade (NICHD ECCRN, 2003; Pianta, 2003), levels of mother-reported internalizing behaviors in kindergarten and first grade (NICHD ECCRN, 2003), and students' engagement in the classroom across all grade levels (Bryant et al., 2002; NICHD ECCRN, 2002, 2005).

Although these processes are important for all students, they may be particularly important for students at risk for school failure. For example, among a group of students who displayed significant behavior and emotional problems in kindergarten, those who were placed in first-grade classrooms offering high levels of emotional support made academic progress at levels similar to their low-risk peers, whereas high-risk students placed in classrooms offering lower levels of emotional support fell further behind their low-risk peers (Hamre & Pianta, 2005). These studies demonstrate that emotional support in the classroom uniquely predicts student outcomes, after adjusting for selection effects and prior student functioning.

Classroom Organization

The Classroom Organization domain includes a broad array of classroom processes related to the organization and management of students' behavior, time, and attention in the classroom (Emmer & Stough, 2001). Classrooms function best and provide the most opportunities for learning when students are well-behaved, consistently have things to do, and are interested and engaged in learning tasks. The theoretical underpinnings of this domain include work by developmental psychologists studying how children develop self-regulatory skills (Blair, 2003; Raver, 2004), work by ecological psychologists examining the extent to which these skills are determined by environmental factors (Kounin, 1970), and constructivist theories exploring how young children are best engaged in learning (Bowman & Stott, 1994; Bruner, 1996; Rogoff, 1990; Vygotsky, 1978). The term *self-regulated learning* (Schunk, 2005; Sperling, Howard, & Staley, 2004) often is used to refer to the regulatory skills students need to be successful in classroom settings. This term is defined as "an active constructive process whereby learners set goals for their learning and then attempt to monitor, regulate, and control their cognition, motivation, and behavior, guided and constrained by their goals and the contextual features in the environment" (Pintrich, 2000, p. 453). A point of emphasis across this definition and the work of other ecological and process–product researchers is that the development and expression of regulatory skills is highly dependent on the classroom environment (Anderson, Evertson, & Emmer, 1980; Emmer & Stough, 2001; Kounin, 1970; Pintrich, 2000; Sanford & Evertson, 1981; Soar & Soar, 1979). At the simplest level, this work suggests that students exhibit better self-regulation in well-regulated classroom environments. The CLASS framework incorporates three dimensions of this classroom-level regulation:

- Behavior Management: How effectively teachers monitor, prevent, and redirect behavior

- Productivity: How well the classroom runs with respect to routines and the degree to which teachers organize activities and directions so that maximum time can be spent in learning activities

- Instructional Learning Formats: How teachers facilitate activities and provide interesting materials so that students are engaged and learning opportunities are maximized

Each of these dimensions captures a distinct aspect of classroom organization that has demonstrated associations with children's learning. With regard to behavior management, classrooms with positive strategies for preventing and redirecting behavior tend to have students who make greater academic progress (Good & Grouws, 1977; Soar & Soar, 1979). In addition, intervention studies provide evidence that teachers who adopt these types of practices after training are more likely than teachers in control groups to have students who are engaged and learning (Emmer & Stough, 2001; Evertson, Emmer, Sanford, & Clements, 1983; Evertson & Harris, 1999). In terms of productivity, early work by process–product researchers has focused attention on the importance of time management, providing consistent evidence that students are most engaged in productive classrooms and that this engagement, in turn, is directly associated with student learning (Brophy & Evertson, 1976; Coker, Medley, & Soar, 1980; Good & Grouws, 1977; Stallings, 1975; Stallings, Cory, Fairweather, & Needels, 1978). In fact, in their review of teacher behavior and student achievement, Brophy and Good (1986) concluded that the link between the *quantity* of time spent on instruction and student achievement was the most consistently replicated finding of process–product researchers. Finally, for students to learn they must not only have something to do but also must be effectively engaged and interested in the instructional activities provided to them as well (Yair, 2000). Consistent with constructivist theories that guide much of early childhood practice (Bowman & Stott, 1994; Bruner, 1996; Rogoff, 1990; Vygotsky, 1978), when teachers provide high-quality learning formats, students are not just *passively* engaged in learning but are *active* participants in the learning experience. Taken together, these dimensions of classroom organization set the stage for learning in preschool to third-grade classrooms.

Instructional Support

The theoretical foundation for the CLASS conceptualization of instructional support comes primarily from research on children's cognitive and language development (e.g., Catts, Fey, Zhang, & Tomblin, 1999; Fujiki, Brinton, & Clarke, 2002; Romberg, Carpenter, & Dremock, 2005; Taylor, Pearson, Peterson, & Rodriguez, 2003; Vygotsky, 1991; Wharton-McDonald, Pressley, & Hampston, 1998). This literature highlights the distinction between simply learning facts and gaining usable knowledge—learning how facts are interconnected, organized, and conditioned on one another (National Research Council, 1999)—noting that gaining usable knowledge is the more important of the two when it comes to cognitive development. The development of *metacognitive skills,* or the awareness and understanding of one's thinking processes, also is critical to children's academic development (Veenman, Kok, & Blöte, 2005; Williams, Blythe, & White, 2002). A child's ability to develop metacognitive skills is contingent on the opportunities that adults provide to express existing skills and scaffold more complex ones (Davis & Miyake, 2004; Skibbe, Behnke, & Justice, 2004; Vygotsky, 1991). Thus, as with the other CLASS domains, interactions between adults and children are the key mechanism through which instructional support is provided to children in the early years of schooling. As a result, the CLASS Instructional Support domain does not focus on the content of curriculum or learning activities but rather on the ways in which teachers implement whichever curriculum they are using to effectively support cognitive and language development. The CLASS has three dimensions that focus on instructional support:

- Concept Development: How teachers use instructional discussions and activities to promote students' higher-order thinking skills in contrast to a focus on rote instruction

- Quality of Feedback: How teachers extend students' learning through their responses to students' ideas, comments, and work

- Language Modeling: The extent to which teachers facilitate and encourage students' language

These dimensions together, and Quality of Feedback in particular, form an index of the instructional value of the classroom that predicts to student academic functioning in the areas of literacy and general knowledge (Howes et al., in press), with indications that this association is a result of increased student engagement in the activity (NICHD ECCRN, 2003).

As with emotional support, there is some evidence that these instructional processes may be particularly important for students at risk for school failure. In one study, students identified as at risk based on low levels of maternal education who were placed in first-grade classrooms offering moderate to high instructional quality displayed academic achievement at a level commensurate with their low-risk peers, whereas those students in low instructional quality classrooms fell further behind (Hamre & Pianta, 2005).

USES OF THE CLASS

The CLASS provides a mechanism through which researchers, policymakers, and practitioners can collect standardized information on the quality of classroom environments from preschool through third grade. Uses of the CLASS include the following:

Research

The CLASS may be used in large or small studies of young students in which researchers want a measure of classroom processes that are 1) linked to students' concurrent school performance and 2) associated with students' development and behavior over time. The CLASS has been used successfully as a part of large research projects documenting the quality of classroom environments across the early grades as well as in evaluation studies seeking to determine whether school-based programs affect classroom processes.

Accountability Efforts

The unprecedented level of investment in and attention to early education has taken place in the context of a policy climate that emphasizes accountability. In particular, when public funds are spent for education, educational providers are increasingly held responsible for their contribution to children's academic and social development. Accountability assessments typically rest on direct evaluation of students. Adopting policies and practices that view direct assessment of students as the only means for ensuring accountability of early education and elementary classrooms is markedly limited for young students for a number of reasons. Direct assessment of young students is known to be less reliable and valid than direct assessment of older students, in large part because younger students' competencies are fairly unstable and situationally dependent (La Paro & Pianta, 2000). Furthermore, because the competencies of students are in large part dependent on the quality of their experiences in educational settings, it makes sense to assess, for accountability purposes, the quality of those settings (Pianta, 2003). In short, when determining accountability in early education classrooms, it may be better to focus on developmental inputs rather than outputs. The CLASS allows for a direct assessment of these inputs.

Program Planning and Evaluation

For programs seeking to improve the quality of their classroom offerings, the CLASS provides a standardized mechanism for assessing classroom-level factors that are amenable to intervention. For example, by administering the CLASS in all K–3 classrooms in a district, administrators may identify systemwide strengths and develop plans for making systematic improvements in areas of weakness. Districts may find that their teachers display high-quality emotional supports and organization but are weaker than teachers in other districts in the instructional areas. They may use that information to plan for a set of workshops aimed at improving teacher knowledge and implementation of high-quality instructional strategies.

Professional Development and Supervision

The CLASS may be used to provide teachers with direct feedback about their actual classroom practices. Teachers can be observed and provided with feedback at regular intervals during the school year. Using the CLASS in this way allows teachers to get feedback about the dimensions of their teaching that are associated with more positive social and academic development for students. In addition, they are given an objective and concrete measurement of their areas of strength and weakness as well as their improvements over the course of the year. The CLASS also can be used as a training tool for preservice teachers by providing them with a framework for understanding the components of their teaching that really matter for students as well as by providing a mechanism for systematic feedback and support throughout their training and early careers. Finally, the CLASS can serve as the basis for new models of in-service training that break away from the traditional workshop model by focusing on providing teachers with on-going, flexible, individualized, and collaborative support to improve their interactions with students (e.g., MyTeachingPartner system, http://www.myteachingpartner.net).

CLASS TRAINING

The previous section outlined some of the ways the CLASS can be used to assess classroom processes in preschool to third-grade classrooms. Potential users include researchers, teachers, principals, school psychologists, and educational consultants.

Reliable use of the CLASS tool requires training. The level of training required depends on the intended use of the system. It is essential that all individuals interested in using the CLASS to collect standardized data on classrooms or for research, accountability, or evaluation purposes attend official training workshops. Learn to fairly and accurately assess teacher–student interactions using the CLASS tool. Attend one of Teachstone's training programs to become a certified CLASS observer or affiliate trainer. Find out more and register for a Teachstone training at: http://www.teachstone.com/training-programs/.

If the CLASS is being used for research or evaluative purposes, it also is important that regular checks on reliability occur after initial training. Conducting regular "double coding" sessions during which at least two observers code the same classroom observation or videotape and check their codes for consistency is highly recommended. In addition, holding regular meetings during which observers code videotaped segments together can help keep people coding consistently. Finally, it is recommended that all observers watch several refresher/drift segments at least once a year after training or prior to each data collection wave to ensure a high degree of reliability with the CLASS manual and master coders.

Observing Classrooms with the CLASS

CHAPTER TWO

This chapter describes the recommended procedure for using the CLASS® in live observation. Ways to use the CLASS to code from videotape and variations in observational strategies when the observer wants the scores to be focused on one teacher, rather than the whole classroom, also are briefly reviewed. These procedures may be adapted to fit the individual needs of a project, but any adaptations should keep the following principles in mind:

- Maximizing the number of observations will increase reliability of measurement.

- Both structured and unstructured times of the school day are important to observe.

Unlike discrete behavioral coding, the CLASS requires the observer to derive one score for each dimension per observation cycle based on the degree to which certain behavioral markers characterize the classroom during that cycle. A score ranging from 1 (minimally characteristic) to 7 (highly characteristic) is given for each dimension and represents the extent to which that dimension is characteristic of that classroom. Each *cycle* of observation consists of a 20-minute period during which the observer watches classroom interaction (mostly focused on the teacher) and takes notes followed by a 10-minute period for recording codes. To complete the ratings, the observer must make *judgments* based on the range, frequency, intention, and tone of interpersonal and individual behavior during the observation time.

GENERAL LIVE OBSERVATION PROCEDURE

The entire CLASS observation typically starts at the beginning of the school day and continues throughout the morning for at least 2 hours. However, the observation can be scheduled to begin later in the day, as desired by the project. Prior to the observation, the observer should discuss with the teacher the schedule for the day and use that information to plan the observation so as to maximize the number of 30-minute cycles that can be obtained. The observer should conduct the observation according to the following rules:

- Observation starts at the time the school day begins, according to the teacher, or at another predetermined time.

- Coding then proceeds using the 30-minute cycle (i.e., 20-minute observe, 10-minute record) until the end of the observation..

- A minimum of four cycles should be obtained. Please note that the Scoring Summary Sheet included with the six Observation Sheets contains space for recording six cycles.

The observation procedure requires the observer to watch, without interruption, activity in the classroom for a period of 20 minutes. During this time, the observer should watch the *who, what,* and *how* of everything that happens at the classroom level, with particular attention to the teachers' instructional interactions and behaviors.

The Observation Sheets have space next to each dimension for the observer to jot down notes to help him or her assign a rating score at the end of each observation cycle. Notes *must* be taken for each dimension during every observation cycle. These notes form the basis for coding and will help observers make a judgment about a code. Notes should reflect the key elements of the dimension and not extraneous information. Notetaking typically helps the coder focus on these key aspects of the interaction they are watching (see the filled-in Observation Sheet on page 16 for an example).

At the end of the 20 minutes of dedicated observation and notetaking, the observer should derive numerical ratings for each of the CLASS dimensions. These ratings are based on the observer's knowledge of the dimension definitions and markers and the written notes that the observer has made during the entire observation window for each dimension. After assigning ratings, the observer should begin a new CLASS cycle.

Classrooms with More than One Teacher/Adult

If multiple adults are present in a classroom, weigh their behaviors according to the number of students with whom they are working, the amount of time they spend with the students, and their responsibility for the activities.

The CLASS dimensions are intended to reflect the value of the classroom environment for all the students in the class or, in other words, the experience of a typical or average student in the class. The dimensions do not target a single student or a single adult but instead are intended to capture the resources present to all students in the classroom. When more than one adult is present in a classroom, the observer must be clear about how to weigh the contributions of each adult when they assign scores on the CLASS dimensions. Most often, the primary teacher will be the focus of the codes. The primary teacher is that individual who is ultimately responsible for everything that happens in the classroom and, in most cases, is leading the interaction being viewed.

If another adult is present in a classroom, he or she is likely a paid teacher's aide, a parent volunteer, or another teacher (i.e., co-teacher). In these cases, observers must use their judgment to decide how to balance their observation time and the resulting codes. Again, the primary principle to remember is that the CLASS codes should reflect the experiences of the typical or average student in the classroom. If most of the students are working under the direction of one adult and a few students are working with another adult, the observer should code the teacher working with the majority of the students. If students are working in small groups and a separate adult is leading each group, the observer should spend time watching each group and code the average of these experiences over the whole 20 minutes, across the groups. If the primary teacher is leading the activity by him- or herself while the second adult is making copies, code the primary teacher's interactions. If the second adult is "floating" in the group while the teacher is leading, the codes, again, should be based primarily on the lead teacher's behavior. If the second adult has complete responsibility for a period of time while the teacher sits at his or her desk, code according to what the second adult is doing.

The CLASS codes are derived based on the behavior of *all* of the adults in the room during a given cycle. In classrooms with multiple adults, it can be assumed that the primary teacher is orchestrating the classroom activities and sanctions all adult interactions with the students. The other adults act as his or her proxies and help maintain the classroom climate in terms of the amount of allowable contact with and between students, academic support to the students, and the amount of control exercised in the classroom.

Rules for What to Observe and Terminating a Cycle

For the most part, observers should watch and code nearly all of the activities that take place in the classroom. If necessary, however, observers may follow the students and teacher outside to code an activity (e.g., for a walk or a science discovery lesson). Observers should terminate observation and not assign codes during recess and outdoor free time. All other periods—music, art, transitions, language arts and/or academics, free choice, and centers—should be coded. Depending on the setting and goals of observation, the observer may choose to observe during snack and mealtime as well. In many early childhood settings, students receive a good deal of instruction during these times— a lot of teaching can occur while students wash their hands and get ready for snack.

If the teacher ends an activity and the students go to recess in the middle of the observation portion of a cycle, the observer should stop observing. Ratings still can be assigned to the CLASS codes based on what the observer has observed up to that point provided that 10 minutes of the observation have been completed. The ratings will be based on what was observed during that 10-minute period.

If the observation cycle is terminated before 10 minutes of observation have occurred, the next observation period should be started once the classroom activity fits the eligible observation description above. For example, if the students return from recess and start getting ready for art instruction, observation can begin during the transition. It is fine, and in fact desirable, to observe during the transition back to the room.

Challenges for the Observer

The CLASS requires observers to make a series of judgments. Although very detailed behavioral markers in the manual, as well as the observers' experience during CLASS training, guide these judgments, observers should keep in mind several important challenges while using the CLASS.

Remaining Objective

Over the course of a complete visit, the observer must guard against injecting external explanations for what he or she sees taking place within the classroom. The visitor must remain true to the individual dimensions. For example, the observer may be tempted to make allowances for the time of day. Thoughts such as "The teacher must be tired considering she has all these tough kids" must not be considered in coding. The dimension and its markers remain stable. The numerical ratings change based on behaviors observed.

When assigning scores, it is imperative to base codes on the written descriptions of the dimensions. Observers should not adjust their codes upward or downward based on any information other than what they have observed in the classroom. It is a common inclination to inflate ratings because observers take the perspective of the teacher. "Oh, she didn't really mean to do that. She just didn't see who really was at fault." Or, "He would have taught the lesson better if the overhead projector had been working properly. I've had things like that happen lots of time. He didn't really mean to be so negative." Perspective taking such as this may cause the observer to adjust the codes to explain more positively what takes place at any given time in the classroom. This should be minimized as much as possible. In addition, the observer should be careful not to adjust ratings based solely on the activity provided for the students. For example, if the teacher is conducting a rote lesson and asks one good Concept Development question, the coder should not adjust the score significantly higher for this because "she did as much as she could with this lesson." The descriptions of dimensions within the manual should always be the basis for assigning scores.

Another area in which observers must be careful to remain objective is in the tendency to develop initial impressions of teachers and to look for evidence confirming these initial impressions. This tendency often causes observers to miss important behaviors that may disconfirm these initial impressions. It is sometimes helpful for the observer to consciously reflect on his or her initial impression a few minutes into the observation and then make an active effort to look for disconfirming evidence. In addition, while the observer is reviewing notes prior to scoring—particularly if all of his or her notes reflect one end of the dimension—he or she should spend a minute reading through the other end of the dimension to see if that cues any thoughts about behaviors he or she may have seen but failed to record.

Independence of Cycles

Another challenge for the observer is to record the ratings accurately without regard to how each dimension was scored in previous cycles. Each cycle must be considered independently of the others with no expectation or need for change or stability. Any pattern in the ratings across time should occur naturally and must be external to the observer's manipulation. Often, there may be little change within one lesson or across lessons with the same teacher in the same classroom. The observer may sense that he or she is responsible for this apparent redundancy or even that, at times, he or she is just giving the same ratings over and over again. There is no expectation that the ratings must vary from cycle to cycle to be considered accurate or to document that the observer is not in what might feel like a *response bias.* There is, in fact, no expectation that an average teacher in one classroom would change greatly across the morning, for example. Changes are more likely to occur when students experience different class groupings, different teachers, different subject materials, or different classrooms or across different students in different schools.

Weighing Single Incidents

Care should be taken not to allow a single incident to be given too much weight in an overall rating. In general, specific incidents that are markers for the different dimensions should be noted and contribute to the rating, but care should be taken that the rating characterizes the whole observation period and not a single occurrence. The observer should make sure that he or she mentally reviews the entire observation segment prior to giving a rating. For example, a classroom should not receive a rating of 1 for Productivity if the teacher takes a brief moment to look for a book or has a brief conversation at the door with another adult. Because these events have occurred, the teacher should not receive a 7, but the teacher's behavior during the entire segment must be evaluated and considered in the rating.

Exemplars

For each rating category (i.e., high, middle, and low) on all of the dimensions, examples are included in the form of statements. Remember that these are only examples and everything in the example does not have to be true in order for a classroom to fit into a given rating category. In addition, events and situations may occur in classrooms that are not included in the examples but still fit well within a given rating category for a given dimension. The examples are intended to serve as guidelines but are not an exhaustive list of all behaviors that could fit into a rating category.

Independence of Dimensions

The dimensions are intended to be analytically distinct, although overlap often occurs. It is often the case that an individual incident in a classroom contributes to the scoring on several dimensions; however, each dimension still should be rated independently. It is important for observers to remain objective and guard against adopting an overall picture of a teacher and then spending the observation period looking for confirmation of that impression across dimensions rather than looking for objective evidence of each dimension throughout the observation.

Seeking Perfection

The high-end markers for each dimension reflect good teaching practice; however, to score in the high range a classroom does not have to be perfect. There may be one or two things that are less than ideal in a given observation, but if the overall classroom experience is characterized by the markers at the high end, the classroom should be scored that way. This may be an issue for observers using the CLASS as a professional development tool. Receiving a high score on a dimension does not preclude the usefulness of a discussion with the teacher being observed about her practice in that area. It is often the case that teachers are not aware of exactly what they are doing well; hearing the specifics of their successes might help them to be more intentional and consistent in implementing these practices in the future.

ALTERNATIVE OBSERVATION PROCEDURES

The observation procedures described previously are those typically used for the CLASS. However, the CLASS was designed to work flexibly with other observational procedures as needed for specific projects. We describe a few alternative observational procedures next.

Videotaped Observation Procedure

The CLASS has been validated for use in coding videotapes of classrooms (Mashburn, Hamre, Downer, & Pianta, 2007). Videotaping may be completed by teachers or by outsiders. The general procedures described previously for live coding also apply to coding videotape. Here, the biggest concern is the degree to which the videotape adequately captures the visual and auditory information present in classroom interactions. The following are recommendations for obtaining high-quality videotape:

- During whole- and small-group time, it is a good idea to use digital video cameras that adequately capture sound without having to have a microphone on the teacher. In some cases, however, such as group work or center time, the teacher may be difficult to hear over the hum of the classroom. Experiment with a few options before collecting a lot of videotape. Most modern computers come with software that allows for easy importation of digital video.

- Make sure the teacher (or person doing the taping) tells the students what is happening prior to the first videotaping. The students should be told why they are being videotaped and allowed to share any concerns they may have about the process. Although students sometimes act up for the camera initially, most quickly forget that it is there.

- Start the video prior to the beginning of a lesson and run the videotape during the transition from one activity to another. Often, these nonlesson times provide interesting moments to watch and discuss.

- Use tripods and place the camera in such a way that the teacher and most of the students can be seen clearly. Often, setting up the camera to the side so that the facial expressions of the teachers and students are visible is most helpful. Move the tripod as needed, but try not to use handheld video as the picture tends to be shaky.

- In the case of group work or centers, focus the video on the primary teacher but occasionally pan the video out to capture the experiences of other students for several minutes at a time.

Using the Class to Observe One Teacher

For some professional development and research purposes, people are interested in obtaining ratings that reflect one teacher rather than the classroom as a whole. In most cases, it is still recommended that observers follow the general procedures described previously. The main classroom teacher is responsible for directing students' experiences in the classroom; therefore, information about interactions that students have with other adults may be important indicators of how the lead teacher has structured the classroom. There are some exceptions to this, however. For example, in work with preservice teachers, the scoring is focused specifically on their interactions with students rather than the interactions between students and the lead teacher. Therefore, if this preservice teacher is only working with a small group of students throughout the observation, only those students' experiences should be coded. Most of the other recommendations made in the general observation procedures section apply to this special use of the CLASS.

SCORING WITH THE CLASS

Scoring with the CLASS results in a set of scores for each classroom representing quality as observed on each dimension during each observation cycle. These scores can be averaged across cycles and consolidated to create domain scores, as described next.

Scoring within Each Cycle

CLASS scoring should be completed immediately after each observation cycle using the Observation Sheet (see Figure 2.1). Observers should give a score for each dimension using the 7-point range outlined in Chapter 3. The dimension descriptions in Chapter 3 provide a thorough explanation of each scale at the low (1, 2), mid- (3, 4, 5), and high (6, 7) ranges. Observers should carefully review the dimension descriptions in Table 2.1 and make their judgments based on them.

It is important to note that although Table 2.1 provides a general scoring guideline, the CLASS is *not a checklist* and observers should view the dimensions as holistic descriptions of classrooms that fall in the low, middle, or high range. In many cases, it is not necessary to see indicators of all markers presented in the description of a given range to assign a score in that range. For example, within Positive Climate it is possible for a classroom to score in the high end, even if positive peer connections are not clearly demonstrated, as long as there are consistent indications of positive teacher–student relationships, positive affect from students and teachers, and mutual respect.

Before scores are assigned, the CLASS observer should carefully review the Dimensions Overview sheet for each dimension (e.g., Positive Climate, Concept Development) to make initial decisions about the extent to which the observed behaviors reflect a low, middle, or high range score. However, we recommend that observers new to the CLASS use the full low-, middle-, and high-range descriptions provided in the manual to make judgments about scores. As users become very familiar with these descriptions, they may use the Dimensions Overview for scoring purposes. However, all users will need to refer back to the detailed descriptions at times. **Because of the highly inferential nature of the CLASS,**

OBSERVATION SHEET

((•CLASS®

Teacher: _601_ Observer: _522_

Start time: _8:30 a.m._ End time: _8:50 a.m._

Number of adults: _2_ Number of children: _15_

CONTENT (circle all; check majority):
(Lit/Lang Arts) ✓   Math   (Science)
Social Studies   Art   Other: _____

FORMAT (circle all; check majority):
Routine   (Whole group)   Individual time
Meals/snacks   Small group   Free choice/centers

Circle appropriate score.

Dimension	Notes	Score
Positive Climate (PC) • Relationships • Positive Affect • Positive Communication • Respect	· Teacher sitting on floor close to students · Matched affect w/girl sitting next to teacher · Lots of praise and verbal affection: "sweety, honey" · Respect > thank you; please; using names	1 2 3 4 **(5)** 6 7
Negative Climate (NC) • Negative Affect • Punitive Control • Sarcasm/Disrespect • Severe Negativity	· None observed	**(1)** 2 3 4 5 6 7
Teacher Sensitivity (TS) • Awareness • Responsiveness • Addresses Problems • Student Comfort	· Surveys kids products and looks to provide assistance · Notices child w/hand raised and comes back to her · Ignores one boy's comment ("looks like American flag") · Responds to most students' questions	1 2 3 4 **(5)** 6 7
Regard for Student Perspectives (RSP) • Flexibility and Student Focus • Support for Autonomy and Leadership • Student Expression • Restriction of Movement	· Teacher directed lesson, but gives kids a role · Rigid > "Geo boards must be on the floor" · Students are responsible for materials · Autonomy w/geo boards, less autonomy in second half	1 2 3 4 **(5)** 6 7
Behavior Management (BM) • Clear Behavior Expectations • Proactive • Redirection of Misbehavior • Student Behavior	· Gives clear directions for lesson · Lots of proactive praise ("Thank you for being ready") · Counts down to let students know time is running out · Reactive to students who aren't sitting criss-cross	1 2 3 **(4)** 5 6 7
Productivity (PD) • Maximizing Learning Time • Routines • Transitions • Preparation	· Constantly involved in an activity · Count-down > routine > kids know what to do · Had to redirect students during transition (unclear routine?) · Kids have materials ready; teacher prepared	1 2 3 4 5 **(6)** 7
Instructional Learning Formats (ILF) • Effective Facilitation • Variety of Modalities and Materials • Student Interest • Clarity of Learning Objectives	· Facilitation > leading the lesson: "turn them, draw a line" · Students have own materials > workbook/geoboards · Students are engaged and involved w/ geoboards, engagement fades with workbook	1 2 3 4 **(5)** 6 7
Concept Development (CD) • Analysis and Reasoning • Creating • Integration • Connections to the Real World	· Rote instruction > what does congruent mean? · Some analysis > comparing shapes and sizes · Students produce their own shapes · No real-world connections	1 **(2)** 3 4 5 6 7
Quality of Feedback (QF) • Scaffolding • Feedback Loops • Prompting Thought Processes • Providing Information • Encouragement and Affirmation	· Brief loop around similarities of shapes · Lots of specific feedback: "These 2 sides aren't as long, so not congruent" · Lots of praise > "excellent," "good," "great job, everyone"	1 2 **(3)** 4 5 6 7
Language Modeling (LM) • Frequent Conversation • Open-Ended Questions • Repetition and Extension • Self- and Parallel Talk • Advanced Language	· Peer conversations · Teacher converses w/student next to her · Very little student-to-teacher talk · Advanced language > symmetry and congruent	1 2 3 **(4)** 5 6 7

Figure 2.1.   Filled-in Observation Sheet.

Table 2.1. Dimension descriptions for the CLASS®

Low range		Middle range			High range	
1	2	3	4	5	6	7
The low-range description fits the classroom and/or teacher very well. All, or almost all, relevant indicators in the low range are present.	The low-range description mostly fits the classroom and/or teacher, but there are one or two indicators that are in the middle range.	The middle-range description mostly fits the classroom and/or teacher, but there are one or two indicators in the low range.	The middle-range description fits the classroom and/or teacher very well. All, or almost all, relevant indicators in the middle range are present.	The middle-range description mostly fits the classroom and/or teacher, but there are one or two indicators in the high range.	The high-range description mostly fits the classroom and/or teacher, but there are one or two indicators in the middle range.	The high-range description fits the classroom and/or teacher very well. All, or almost all, relevant indicators in the high range are present.

scores should never be given without referring to the manual. In addition, because of the interactive nature of classrooms, we highly recommend that anyone using the CLASS go through an official training in which they learn to relate the examples given in the manual to actual classroom interactions. Training on master-coded videotape provides invaluable experience and helps users of the CLASS learn, for example, how much Concept Development is enough to earn a score of 7. More information on training is available on the CLASS web site (http://www.classobservation.com).

Getting Composite Scores Across Cycles

To get composite scores across cycles, individual cycle scores for each dimension are averaged across the number of cycles of observations completed. For example, the sample Scoring Summary Sheet in Figure 2.2 contains cycle level scores for each dimension from six observation cycles. Scores within each dimension are averaged and the average score is recorded in the last column of the observation table. On the sample Scoring Summary Sheet, Positive Climate was scored as 5, 5, 5, 7, 6, and 6 across the six cycles. Summing these scores and dividing by the number of cycles (6) yields the average Positive Climate score of 5.67 recorded in the final column of the table. Continue down the column, averaging scores within each domain across all observation cycles.

Obtaining Domain Scores

Once all of the average dimension scores are obtained, the composite domain scores can be calculated: Emotional Support, Classroom Organization, and Instructional Support. These domain scores represent the average of each of the corresponding dimension scores (following the formula provided for each domain; see Scoring Summary Sheet). For example, on the sample Scoring Summary Sheet, shaded boxes indicate dimensions that correspond to each of the CLASS domains. The first four dimensions, Positive Climate

SCORING SUMMARY SHEET

Teacher: __601__   Observer: __522__

Center/ID: __C-22__   Date: __10-5-07__

Start time: __8:00 a.m.__   End time: __10:50 a.m.__

DIRECTIONS

Copy scores from observation sheets. Compute average scores for each dimension by adding cycle scores and then dividing by the number of cycles completed. Finally, compute Domain scores as indicated.

Emotional Support

$$\frac{\underset{\text{PC}}{5.67} + \underset{\text{reversed NC}^1}{6.33} + \underset{\text{TS}}{5.33}}{} $$

$$+ \underset{\text{RSP}}{5.17} \;/4 = \boxed{5.63}$$

¹To reverse NC, subtract average score from 8.

Classroom Organization

$$\frac{\underset{\text{BM}}{6} + \underset{\text{PD}}{5.17} + \underset{\text{ILF}}{5.5}}{}$$

$$/3 = \boxed{5.56}$$

Instructional Support

$$\frac{\underset{\text{CD}}{2.5} + \underset{\text{QF}}{2.33} + \underset{\text{LM}}{2.83}}{}$$

$$/3 = \boxed{2.55}$$

	Cycle 1	Cycle 2	Cycle 3	Cycle 4	Cycle 5	Cycle 6	Average
Number of students	15	15	10	15	12	15	
Number of adults	1	2	2	2	2	2	
Academic content (circle all; check majority)	Lit/Lang Arts, Math, (Social Studies), Science, Art, Other:	√Lit/Lang Arts, Math, Social Studies, (Science), Art, Other:	Lit/Lang Arts, Math, Social Studies, (Science), (Art)√, Other:	Lit/Lang Arts, Math, Social Studies, Science, (Art), Other:	Lit/Lang Arts, Math, (Social Studies), Science, Art, Other:	Lit/Lang Arts, Math, Social Studies, (Science), Art, Other:	
Format (circle all; check majority)	Routine, Meals/Snacks, (Whole group), Free choice/centers, Individual time, (Small groups), Other:	Routine, Meals/Snacks, (Whole group), Free choice/centers, Individual time, Small groups, Other:	Routine, Meals/Snacks, Whole group, (Free choice/centers), (Individual time), Small groups, Other:	Routine, Meals/Snacks, Whole group, Free choice/centers, Individual time, Small groups, Other:	Routine, Meals/Snacks, (Whole group), Free choice/centers, Individual time, Small groups, Other:	Routine, Meals/Snacks, Whole group, Free choice/centers, Individual time, (Small groups), Other:	
Start time	8:00	8:30	9:00	9:30	10:00	10:30	
End time	8:20	8:50	9:20	9:50	10:20	10:50	
PC	1 2 3 4 ⑤ 6 7	1 2 3 4 ⑤ 6 7	1 2 3 4 ⑤ 6 7	1 2 3 4 5 6 ⑦	1 2 3 4 5 6 ⑦	1 2 3 4 5 6 ⑦	5.67
NC	① 2 3 4 5 6 7	① 2 3 4 5 6 7	① 2 3 4 5 6 7	1 ② 3 4 5 6 7	① 2 3 4 5 6 7	① 2 3 4 5 6 7	1.67
TS	1 2 3 4 ⑤ 6 7	1 2 3 4 ⑤ 6 7	1 2 3 4 5 6 ⑦	1 2 3 ④ 5 6 7	1 2 3 4 ⑤ 6 7	1 2 3 4 5 ⑥ 7	5.33
RSP	1 2 3 ④ 5 6 7	1 2 3 4 ⑤ 6 7	1 2 3 4 5 6 ⑦	1 2 3 ④ 5 6 7	1 2 3 4 5 ⑥ 7	1 2 3 4 ⑤ 6 7	5.17
BM	1 2 3 4 5 6 ⑦	1 2 3 ④ 5 6 7	1 2 3 4 5 6 ⑦	1 2 3 4 5 ⑥ 7	1 2 3 4 ⑤ 6 7	1 2 3 4 5 6 ⑦	6
PD	1 2 3 4 ⑤ 6 7	1 2 3 4 5 ⑥ 7	1 2 3 4 ⑤ 6 7	1 2 3 4 5 ⑥ 7	1 2 3 4 ⑤ 6 7	1 2 3 4 ⑤ 6 7	5.17
ILF	1 2 3 ④ 5 6 7	1 2 3 4 ⑤ 6 7	1 2 3 ④ 5 6 7	1 2 3 4 5 6 ⑦	1 2 3 4 ⑤ 6 7	1 2 3 4 ⑤ 6 7	5.5
CD	① 2 3 4 5 6 7	1 ② 3 4 5 6 7	① 2 3 4 5 6 7	1 2 ③ 4 5 6 7	1 2 3 ④ 5 6 7	1 2 ③ 4 5 6 7	2.5
QF	1 ② 3 4 5 6 7	1 2 ③ 4 5 6 7	1 2 ③ 4 5 6 7	1 2 ③ 4 5 6 7	① 2 3 4 5 6 7	1 2 ③ 4 5 6 7	2.33
LM	① 2 3 4 5 6 7	1 2 3 ④ 5 6 7	1 2 3 ④ 5 6 7	1 ② 3 4 5 6 7	1 ② 3 4 5 6 7	1 ② 3 4 5 6 7	2.83

Figure 2.2. Filled-in Scoring Summary Sheet.

(PC), Negative Climate (NC), Teacher Sensitivity (TS), and Regard for Student Perspective (RSP), comprise the Emotional Support domain. The next three dimensions, Behavior Management (BM), Productivity (PD), and Instructional Learning formats (ILF) comprise the Classroom Organization domain. The following three dimensions, Concept Development (CD), Quality of Feedback (QF), and Language Modeling (LM) comprise the Instructional Support domain.

Average dimension scores are transferred to the corresponding spaces within each Domain score box on the left side of the Scoring Summary Sheet. Note that the average score for Negative Climate (NC) is reversed; to reverse the score, subtract the average NC score from 8, and then record this value in the space provided. Calculate the average of the dimension scores within each Domain and enter the average in the space provided. For example, on the sample Scoring Summary Sheet, the sum of the PC, NC, TS, and RSP scores is divided by 4, and the average score for the Emotional Support domain is calculated as 5.63. Note that although Emotional Support is comprised of four dimensions, the following two domains (Classroom Organization and Instructional Support) are each comprised of three dimensions, so the sum of their dimension scores is divided by 3.

CLASS Dimensions

This chapter provides additional information on each of the CLASS® dimensions. Pages 22, 44, and 63 provide a summary of the dimensions in each domain. These summaries are followed by short overviews of each of the dimensions along with concise descriptions of the low-, middle-, and high-range indicators that go along with each dimension. The CLASS observer should use these short overview pages to become familiar with the various dimensions but not for scoring purposes. Refer to the detailed descriptions for scoring purposes.

Throughout this chapter are extensive descriptions of the low-, middle-, and high-range indicators for each dimension. Observers should refer to these comprehensive descriptions when scoring the CLASS.

New users of the CLASS should review this chapter thoroughly. Again, it is helpful to first read each overview page and make an initial judgment about whether the classroom falls in the low, middle, or high range, then to turn to the relevant low-, middle-, or high-range description and carefully read that section. (Placing tabs on the beginning page of each dimension may facilitate easy access during scoring.) If the description does not quite fit, read the other descriptions for that dimension before scoring.

Positive Climate

Reflects the emotional connection between the teacher and students and among students and the warmth, respect, and enjoyment communicated by verbal and nonverbal interactions

Negative Climate

Reflects the overall level of expressed negativity in the classroom; the frequency, quality, and intensity of teacher and peer negativity are key to this scale

Teacher Sensitivity

Encompasses the teacher's awareness of and responsivity to students' academic and emotional needs; high levels of sensitivity facilitate students' ability to actively explore and learn because the teacher consistently provides comfort, reassurance, and encouragement

Regard for Student Perspectives

Captures the degree to which the teacher's interactions with students and classroom activities place an emphasis on students' interests, motivations, and points of view and encourage student responsibility and autonomy

Positive Climate

Reflects the emotional connection between the teacher and students and among students and the warmth, respect, and enjoyment communicated by verbal and nonverbal interactions

	Low (1,2)	Mid (3,4,5)	High (6,7)
Relationships • Physical proximity • Shared activities • Peer assistance • Matched affect • Social conversation	There are few, if any, indications that the teacher and students enjoy warm, supportive relationships with one another.	There are some indications that the teacher and students enjoy warm, supportive relationships with one another.	There are many indications that the teacher and students enjoy warm, supportive relationships with one another.
Positive affect • Smiling • Laughter • Enthusiasm	There are no or few displays of positive affect by the teacher and/or students.	There are sometimes displays of positive affect by the teacher and/or students.	There are frequent displays of positive affect by the teacher and/or students.
Positive communication • Verbal affection • Physical affection • Positive expectations	There are rarely positive communications, verbal or physical, among teachers and students.	There are sometimes positive communications, verbal or physical, among teachers and students.	There are frequently positive communications, verbal or physical, among teachers and students.
Respect • Eye contact • Warm, calm voice • Respectful language • Cooperation and/or sharing	The teacher and students rarely, if ever, demonstrate respect for one another.	The teacher and students sometimes demonstrate respect for one another.	The teacher and students consistently demonstrate respect for one another.

Low Positive Climate (1, 2)

There are few, if any, indications that the teacher and students enjoy warm, support-ive relationships with one another. The teacher and students do not appear to be con-nected to one another in any meaningful way. They may appear distant, not listen carefully when others are talking, and/or lack warmth and genuineness in interactions with one another. The teacher remains physically distant from students and does not join in activi-ties with the students. Few students interact with one another during structured or unstructured activities, and a lack of shared smiles, warmth, or concern among students is notable. For example, during small-group work, one student cannot find her workbook and is upset; however, the other students in her group fail to show concern or make any effort to help. The teacher and students do not appear interested in what they are doing and appear to get little pleasure out of interactions with one another. The teacher's affect does not match and is not connected to the affect of the students. For example, the students may laugh or smile while the teacher reads a book to the class, but the teacher's affect remains flat, or the teacher may give a student a compliment but the student fails to respond in a positive manner (e.g., smiling, looking at teacher). The teacher may be very friendly and social with other adults, but interactions with the students may be strained or contrived. The teacher does not attempt to connect with the students on a personal level through talking with them about their lives outside the classroom. If students tell the teacher personal things (e.g., "My mom took me to the swimming pool last night," "My friend broke his arm yesterday"), then the teacher either ignores them or fails to develop the topic into a meaningful conversation by saying something perfunctory such as, "That's nice" or "I'm sorry to hear that," with little affect or interest communicated to the student. Students also fail to engage in this type of informal, social conversation with one another.

There are no or few displays of positive affect by the teacher and/or students. Teacher and student affect is flat with only very rare occasions of smiling or laughter. The teacher often appears to be preoccupied or simply going through the motions. She shows little, if any, enthusiasm for her job as a teacher. Students may appear to be listening or participating, but there is a notable lack of enthusiasm and enjoyment as they go about their day, as indicated by flat affect.

There are rarely positive communications, verbal or physical, among teachers and students. The teacher does not provide verbal affection (e.g., positive feedback, praise) to students such as, "Nice job" or "I really enjoyed working with you all today; it was fun to see all the things you were learning." The teacher makes no attempts to use appropriate physical affection in interactions with students, or these attempts are not accepted by stu-dents. For example, the teacher may put her arm around a student and the student pulls away. Students do not, or rarely, make positive comments to or use physical affection with one another. The teacher does not communicate positive expectations for students (e.g., "I know you can do it," "You guys are really smart and I know you can figure this out").

The teacher and students rarely, if ever, demonstrate respect for one another. Respect is communicated through words and nonverbal behaviors. At the low end of this dimension, a teacher's interactions with students may be perfunctory; she may not make eye contact as she speaks to them. Students also may not show this respect to one another. For example, as one student is responding to the teacher's question during a small-group lesson, the other students may be looking around the room or talking to one another. The teacher fails to use a warm, calm voice when talking with students. The teacher and students do not use words that communicate respect (e.g., thank you, please, you are welcome) or a respectful tone of voice. The teacher and students infrequently address one another by name or frequently call each other by the incorrect name. Students may appear reluctant to cooperate, work together, or share materials with one another.

Middle-Range Positive Climate (3, 4, 5)

There are some indications that the teacher and students enjoy warm, supportive relationships with one another. The teacher and students generally appear to have positive regard for one another, but there may be a constrained element to interactions at times. The teacher sometimes is in close physical proximity to students and other times is not. The teacher may sometimes join in activities with students but other times remains more distant. For example, the teacher may seem to enjoy working with a small group of students (exhibits interested and positive tone of voice and close physical proximity); however, when the class makes the transition to whole-group instruction, the teacher appears less connected (not engaging with individual students, failing to demonstrate enthusiasm or positive demeanor). The students in this classroom generally have positive interactions with peers, but these interactions may not occur spontaneously or among the majority of students. If one student is confused during a group activity, then one of the other students may take notice and try to support and help the student; however, there is not a shared attempt by all of the students to help one another. Likewise, some peers may appear quite connected to each other, whereas others seem fairly distant. The teacher's affect sometimes matches the affect of the students and at other times does not. There may be some evidence of social conversation among the teacher and students, but these conversations are very brief and the teacher ends them before the student. For example, a student may initiate a social conversation (e.g., "I went to the library with my mom yesterday") and the teacher may respond or ask one or two questions of the student (e.g., "Did you get any books?" "How was it?") but does not appear genuinely interested in what the student has to say. In addition, students appear only mildly interested in what their peers are saying.

There are sometimes displays of positive affect by the teacher and/or students. The teacher may display positive affect with some students but not as much with others or demonstrate extremely positive affect during some observational periods but less positive affect during other periods. Although, at times, the teacher and student may be observed laughing or smiling, at other times teacher and/or student affect is flat. The teacher and/or students sometimes show enthusiasm and appear to enjoy their time in the classroom but other times appear less enthusiastic or simply seem to be going through the motions.

There are sometimes positive communications, verbal or physical, among teachers and students. There may be occasional displays of verbal or physical affection, but these are not typical. The teacher may sometimes provide positive communications (e.g., praise, positive feedback), but at other times, these communications are not evident. The teacher may occasionally communicate positive expectations for students such as, "I know you can do this," but these communications are infrequent or are only communicated to a single student.

The teacher and students sometimes demonstrate respect for one another. The teacher sometimes shows respect for the students by establishing eye contact with them when speaking but other times does not. In a similar regard, students sometimes may pay attention to what their peers are saying but other times fail to do so. Sometimes the teacher's voice is warm and calm; other times, it is less so. The teacher and students sometimes use words that connote respect such as "please" and "thank you," but these words are not used consistently and do not always sound sincere. The teacher and students sometimes refer to each other by name and other times do not. Some students cooperate with one another and share materials, whereas others do not.

High Positive Climate (6, 7)

There are many indications that the teacher and students enjoy warm, supportive relationships with one another. There is strong evidence of an emotional connection between the teacher and students, and the teacher and students clearly enjoy being with one another. The teacher often is in close physical proximity to the students and freely joins in the students' activities. Students appear interested in spending time with one another and appear comfortable with close physical proximity to one another. They may actively seek opportunities to interact with one another and work together when given the opportunity (e.g., during group projects, free time, or centers). Students appear to be interested in helping one another and show concern and a desire to help if one of their peers is upset or confused. Please note that a classroom may be coded at the high end of Positive Climate without observing positive connections between peers if there are no opportunities for peer interaction during the observation period, as may be the case if the teacher is involved in whole-group instruction during the entire period. However, to be scored in the high range in this case, there must be clear evidence of the other markers of Positive Climate; observers should note that even within these whole-group lessons, students appear comfortable with one another. There is a match between teacher and student affect; when the students show excitement and enthusiasm, so does the teacher, and the teacher smiles and laughs with the students. If a teacher makes an attempt at physical contact (e.g., putting her arm around a student, patting a student on the back) or provides verbal support (e.g., "You are working really hard today," "I like the way you are thinking!"), that positive affect is generally returned and/or accepted. There may be frequent social conversations between the teacher and students or among students. When a teacher is having social conversations with students, she appears genuinely interested as evidenced by behaviors such as looking at the student, getting down to their level, asking follow-up questions, and using an interested tone of voice. Similar levels of interest are shown when students have social conversations with one another.

There are frequent displays of positive affect by the teacher and/or students. The classroom feels like a warm, pleasant place to be with many instances of enthusiasm including laughter or smiling among the teacher and students. The teacher displays general positive affect throughout the observation. The students give the impression that they are in a pleasant environment and that they enjoy spending time in the classroom. The teacher and students frequently smile and laugh and display enthusiasm in their classroom work and work with one another.

There are frequently positive communications, verbal or physical, among teachers and students. The teacher freely responds to students' efforts and participation in activities and lessons with positive comments such as, "What a good idea. Did everyone hear what James said just now?" or "Look at your handwriting. I can tell you have worked really hard on that!" Students also may spontaneously make these types of positive comments to one another. For example, as students are working on drawing pie charts at their desks, one student may look over to his neighbor and spontaneously say, "Wow, that is a great chart, you do really neat drawings." Or, in a group book discussion, students may reinforce each other's comments and build upon them, saying, "I agree with Tony, and I would like to add to what he said." This indicates that students are both listening and responding to peers with respect. The students and teacher in this classroom may appear comfortable freely giving and receiving physical affection, although this is not necessary for a rating in the high range. The teacher also communicates positive expectations for the students such as, "I know you are going to do a great job on this," "This is a cool project and I know we will really enjoy it," or "You are really smart, and I know you are going to be able to figure this out."

The teacher and students consistently demonstrate respect for one another. The teacher demonstrates respect for the students by establishing eye contact when speaking to them. Students also indicate respect for one another by listening to each other. For example, when one student is answering a question during a whole-group lesson, the other students pay attention, look at the student, and so forth. When speaking to the students, the teacher consistently has a warm and calm voice. The teacher and students use language that communicates respect, such as "please," "thank you," and "you are welcome" and frequently call or refer to one another by name. The students in this classroom are cooperative, wait patiently in line, and share materials.

Negative Climate[2]

Reflects the overall level of expressed negativity in the classroom; the frequency, quality, and intensity of teacher and peer negativity are key to this scale

	Low (1,2)	Mid (3,4,5)	High (6,7)
Negative affect • Irritability • Anger • Harsh voice • Peer aggression • Disconnected or escalating negativity	The teacher and students do not display strong negative affect and only rarely, if ever, display mild negativity.	The classroom is characterized by mild displays of irritability, anger, or other negative affect by the teacher and/or the students.	The classroom is characterized by consistent irritability, anger, or other negative affect by the teacher and/or the students.
Punitive control • Yelling • Threats • Physical control • Harsh punishment	The teacher does not yell or make threats to establish control.	The teacher occasionally uses expressed negativity such as threats or yelling to establish control.	The teacher repeatedly yells at students or makes threats to establish control.
Sarcasm/disrespect • Sarcastic voice/statement • Teasing • Humiliation	The teacher and students are not sarcastic or disrespectful.	The teacher and/or students are occasionally sarcastic or disrespectful.	The teacher and/or students are repeatedly sarcastic or disrespectful.
Severe negativity • Victimization • Bullying • Physical punishment	There are no instances of severe negativity between the teacher and students.	There are no instances of severe negativity between the teacher and students.	There are instances of severe negativity between the teacher and students or among the students.

---

[2]Negative Climate is scaled in the opposite direction of the other CLASS scales. Higher negativity indicates lower quality.

Low Negative Climate (1, 2)

The teacher and students do not display strong negative affect and only rarely, if ever, display mild negativity. There are no instances when a teacher displays strong anger or verbal or physical aggression during interactions with students. There may be very mild negativity, such as irritation, but these instances are rare and do not last for an extended period of time. Negativity among students either is absent or occurs rarely, such as a short argument about whose turn it is during a group activity. These instances are brief, and students quickly get back to more positive interactions with one another. Any mild negativity clearly is tied to a specific situation, is alleviated quickly, and does not rise above a very mild level. In this classroom, occasional mild negativity may occur, such as a teacher grimace or a student getting upset with a peer, but these situations are quickly resolved and have a fleeting quality to them. The teacher and students demonstrate the ability to effectively regulate their own negative affect; thus, mild negativity such as student frustration or teacher irritability is dealt with in such a way that it does not escalate to more intense levels. The teacher and the students show the ability to modulate and dampen any negativity once it is expressed.

The teacher does not yell or make threats to establish control. In dealing with students' misbehavior, this teacher remains calm and does not use a negative tone of voice, yell, or threaten students.

The teacher and students are not sarcastic or disrespectful. This teacher does not make sarcastic or disrespectful comments (e.g., "Did I ask you to open your book, yes or no?"), use a sarcastic tone of voice (e.g., "Yeah, you really look like you are ready to join the group," to a student who is not paying attention), or roll his or her eyes. The teacher may engage in a mildly sarcastic comment on a rare occasion (once or twice during the observation), but these mildly negative comments do not characterize his or her typical interactions with students. The teacher does not humiliate, put down, or disgrace students. Similarly, the students are not sarcastic or disrespectful of one another.

There are no instances of severe negativity between the teacher and students. Examples of severe negativity are generally rare in classroom settings but include sustained victimization or bullying of students or a teacher hitting a student. In the presence of such severe negativity, classrooms may be rated in the high range for Negative Climate, even in the absence of other Negative Climate indicators.

Middle-Range Negative Climate (3, 4, 5)

The classroom is characterized by mild displays of irritability, anger, or other negative affect by the teacher and/or the students. The teacher is not consistently negative in his or her interactions with the students, but there are occasions of negativity. There may be one or two examples of moderately negative behavior such as yelling or using a harsh tone of voice or more frequent observations of low-level negativity such as irritation or annoyance that continue for a substantial amount of time. The teacher sometimes appears to have difficulty effectively regulating his or her own negative affect. The teacher may appear to get frustrated or upset with students during difficult moments such as when they are misbehaving, do not understand a lesson or concept, or when there is chaos in the room. In these instances, the teacher's initial irritation may escalate and be expressed more clearly to students before it dissipates. Students in the classroom rarely, if ever, engage in aggressive interactions with one another (e.g., hostile pushing, hitting) but may be observed to engage in milder forms of negativity such as name calling, poking each other, tattling, or taking materials away from one another. These periods of peer negativity may extend for short periods of time before they are resolved but do not escalate into more serious problems. Mild negativity may appear disconnected from any specific event in the classroom; the teacher may express annoyance and irritation to the students without a clear reason. For example, the teacher may walk over to a group of students working together in a focused and productive way on a math activity using unifix cubes and say in an annoyed tone, "You know you guys have dropped about five cubes on the floor. We are in third grade now; this kind of behavior really should not be an issue for us. I don't know what the problem is," and walk away.

The teacher occasionally uses expressed negativity such as threats or yelling to establish control. In dealing with misbehavior, this teacher may very occasionally (once or twice during the observation) use yelling, anger, or threats (e.g., saying in an angry tone of voice, "Because you all have behaved so badly, you have angered me to the point where I am not going to let you go outside for recess at all today unless you shape up right now") as a way to get students attention or gain control. The teacher also occasionally may use mild physical redirection such as gently pushing or pulling to get students to move rather than telling them with words.

The teacher and/or students are occasionally sarcastic or disrespectful. When students answer questions or seek attention from the teacher, the teacher sometimes may make a derogatory remark, roll his or her eyes, or make a grimace, but other times he or she does not display these negative behaviors to the students. The teacher may occasionally humiliate, put down, or disgrace students, but this does not characterize his or her typical behavior. For example, a few times during the observation, the teacher may call out a student's misbehavior in such a way that the student appears to be shamed in front of his peers (e.g., "Daniel did I ask you to do anything else right now? Yes or no? Then what are you doing?"). Students are disrespectful to one another on occasion, and they may be observed teasing one another at times.

There are no instances of severe negativity between the teacher and students. Examples of severe negativity are very rare but include sustained victimization or bullying of students or a teacher hitting a student. In the presence of such severe negativity, classrooms may be rated in the high range for Negative Climate, even in the absence of other Negative Climate indicators.

High Negative Climate (6, 7)

The classroom is characterized by consistent irritability, anger, or other negative affect by the teacher and/or the students. In highly negative classrooms, the teacher appears irritated or annoyed by students much of the time *or* the students are consistently negative in their interactions with one another. The teacher's irritation is clearly communicated to students during his or her interactions with them. For example, when a student volunteers or asks a question, the teacher may criticize or belittle her (e.g., "I can't believe you don't know this by now"), expressing disapproval toward the student's efforts and abilities. The teacher's negative affect and behavior may escalate during interactions with students, such that he or she starts out irritated but becomes increasingly angry as things continue to go poorly. Alternately, the negativity in the classroom (e.g., harsh tone of voice, annoyance with students even when they are not doing anything wrong) may simply be present at a constant level throughout the observation. Negativity at this level is often disconnected from any specific event; the teacher repeatedly expresses annoyance and irritation to students without a clear reason. The teacher takes a negative stance toward his interactions with most students and seems to be looking for things about which to be annoyed. Interactions among students in these classrooms may be aggressive or marked by teasing and fighting. Students in these classrooms may appear sad, angry, or withdrawn; in general, the students seem generally unhappy. Negative interactions among students tend to escalate or are sustained over moderate to long periods of time. It is possible for a classroom to score in the high range without observing negative peer interactions if the quality of teacher–student interactions is globally negative, as reflected in the previously mentioned indicators. Alternately, peer negativity can lead to a high score in the absence of teacher negativity if it is sustained or involves more than one or two students.

The teacher repeatedly yells at students or makes threats to establish control. This teacher is observed to resort to yelling at or punitively threatening students who misbehave. He or she may also engage in physical controls such as pushing or pulling students in an angry way to get them to line up in a straight line as they get ready to leave the classroom, commenting, "I said line up straight. Let's go guys." If a student refuses to stand up when asked, this teacher may yell, "Stand up!" and then pull the student to his or her feet. The teacher attempts to control students by yelling threats at them such as, "You better start behaving or you won't get to go outside today" or "I am getting really tired of your attitude; you better shape up right now or you are going to have to sit here by yourself while everyone else gets to have fun." These punitive controls happen more than once or twice during the observation.

The teacher and/or students are repeatedly sarcastic or disrespectful. Sarcasm can be communicated to students through the teacher's words or tone. For example, after a student provides an incorrect answer to a question, a sarcastic teacher may respond, "Boy, you are really being smart today, aren't you?" The teacher may often humiliate, put down, or disgrace students. Students also may be disrespectful of one another, engaging in frequent relational aggression such as teasing, excluding other students, and so forth.

There are instances of severe negativity between the teacher and students or among the students. In contrast to most areas of the CLASS, one or two instances of very severe negativity may lead to a high-end rating. Examples of severe negativity are very rare but include sustained victimization or bullying of students, a teacher hitting a student, or students physically fighting with one another. Classrooms should score in the high range of negativity if these events occur, even in the absence of other Negative Climate indicators.

Teacher Sensitivity

Encompasses the teacher's awareness of and responsivity to students' academic and emotional needs; high levels of sensitivity facilitate students' ability to actively explore and learn because the teacher consistently provides comfort, reassurance, and encouragement

	Low (1,2)	Mid (3,4,5)	High (6,7)
Awareness • Anticipates problems and plans appropriately • Notices lack of understanding and/or difficulties	The teacher consistently fails to be aware of students who need extra support, assistance, or attention.	The teacher is sometimes aware of students who need extra support, assistance, or attention.	The teacher is consistently aware of students who need extra support, assistance, or attention.
Responsiveness • Acknowledges emotions • Provides comfort and assistance • Provides individualized support	The teacher is unresponsive to or dismissive of students and provides the same level of assistance to all students, regardless of their individual needs.	The teacher is responsive to students sometimes but at other times is more dismissive or unresponsive, matching his or her support to the needs and abilities of some students but not others.	The teacher is consistently responsive to students and matches his or her support to their needs and abilities.
Addresses problems • Helps in an effective and timely manner • Helps resolve problems	The teacher is ineffective at addressing students' problems and concerns.	The teacher is sometimes effective at addressing students' problems and concerns.	The teacher is consistently effective at addressing students' problems and concerns.
Student comfort • Seeks support and guidance • Freely participates • Takes risks	The students rarely seek support, share their ideas with, or respond to questions from the teacher.	The students sometimes seek support from, share their ideas with, or respond to questions from the teacher.	The students appear comfortable seeking support from, sharing their ideas with, and responding freely to the teacher.

Low Teacher Sensitivity (1, 2)

The teacher consistently fails to be aware of students who need extra support, assistance, or attention. Students in this classroom are frequently disengaged, frustrated, or confused because the teacher pays little attention to their needs. The teacher may not move around the classroom or otherwise get in a position where he or she can see what most students are doing during small group or center time, or students may be seated in a large circle that allows several students to be out of range of the teacher. A student may have to raise his or her hand for a very long time or stand waiting for a long time to get the teacher's attention. The teacher may not plan his or her activities or lessons at the appropriate developmental level for the students. He or she may speak "over their heads" or provide activities that are much too difficult for the students without providing adequate help. For example, a teacher may ask students to tell her the steps in resolving a conflict with peers. A few students respond by saying, "You shouldn't fight with other people" and "Everyone should be friends in our class," clearly indicating that they do not understand the question. The teacher keeps repeating the question and eventually tells the students the answer rather than acknowledging their misunderstanding and asking the question in a way that they can understand. The teacher may continue with lessons despite observable evidence that the students do not understand the content. For example, the teacher may be doing a lesson about presidents and the United States government. Each time he asks a question about the role of the president, nobody raises his or her hand or calls out a correct answer. As the teacher continues discussing the duties of the president, the students begin fidgeting and talking and playing with one another. The teacher, low on sensitivity, is not aware of student disengagement and continues with the lesson, asking more questions about the government. The students' confusion and subsequent misbehavior are evidence that the teacher has not planned a lesson that is appropriate for the developmental level of the students. As another example, the teacher may be teaching in lecture format and continue talking without realizing that many students look either openly confused or are completely disengaged because they have gotten lost along the way. The teacher may look at the overhead projector rather than at the students. The teacher low on sensitivity will not be aware of signals indicating that he needs to slow down, provide more examples, or prompt students to ask questions.

The teacher is unresponsive to or dismissive of students and provides the same level of assistance to all students, regardless of their individual needs. When students approach the teacher with questions or the teacher is dismissive, does not pay attention, or says things such as, "I'm busy" or "Don't bug me right now." This teacher may also ignore or cut off students' enthusiasm, efforts to share exciting news, and expressions of feelings. When students are disengaged or express frustration, sadness, or confusion, the teacher ignores them or quickly dismisses their problems without providing comfort, reassurance, or encouragement. Without any teacher attention or response, these students may be observed to have escalating problems. In addition, the teacher may be dismissive of students' emotional expression, particularly negative emotions (e.g., "Stop frowning; it makes me sad to look at you," "I only talk to happy students"). The teacher may try to joke with an unhappy student instead of first acknowledging his or her feelings. This pattern of interactions prevents the development of students' sense of safety in the classroom and does not allow for the students to view the teacher as an emotional resource or secure base. A teacher low on sensitivity also will fail to individualize support to students. For example, one student making a presentation to the class may be able to speak comfortably in front of her peers and, therefore, does not need much teacher assistance. The next student may be very uncomfortable and confused when he stands up to speak, but the teacher simply sits expectantly as she did with the first student, doing nothing to help him along.

The teacher is ineffective at addressing students' problems and concerns. The teacher is not focused on her students' needs and seems out of touch with them to such a degree that even when she tries to help them, the attempts fail to effectively resolve the students' problems. For example, a student may approach the teacher very distressed because she feels that another student was cheating in their science lab. The teacher goes over to the students' lab table and says, "I don't know what is going on here but your group needs to just start over and get along." This does not appropriately acknowledge or address the student's feelings that she was not treated fairly by the other student and therefore does not effectively resolve the student's problem. As another example, two students experiencing a conflict approach the teacher for help, but the teacher is taking attendance and tells them that he is busy and will get to them later. The students are not able to move forward because they are waiting for the teacher to help them resolve their conflict. In addition, ineffectiveness at meeting students' needs often is observed when a student must keep approaching the teacher for help because the real problem has not been resolved.

The students rarely seek support, share their ideas with, or respond to questions from the teacher. Students in classrooms characterized by low teacher sensitivity often have learned that the teacher is not a source of support or reassurance and thus may not seek him or her out when they are having a hard time and need comfort. In these classrooms, many students may look confused or unsure. For example, when completing worksheets, students who do not know what to do or are unsure of how to complete the activity do not ask the teacher for help; instead, they may put their heads down on the table or become engaged in inappropriate activities. The lack of or inconsistent pattern of responsiveness contributes to students not volunteering responses and calling out answers. For example, after reading the daily news during morning meeting, the teacher may ask the students what they think of the news story they just heard; few students, however, are willing to raise their hand or call out a response.

Middle-Range Teacher Sensitivity (3, 4, 5)

The teacher is sometimes aware of students in need of extra support, assistance, or attention. This teacher may appear inconsistently aware of the needs of his or her students. For example, he may seem very clued in to students' academic needs, giving them appropriate tasks, supporting their learning, and so forth, but be less aware of students' emotional functioning. A teacher in this range may be conducting a lesson on hearing the different sounds in words and take time to make sure that students understand the concepts, but he or she may miss the fact that several students have recently gotten into an argument and are so upset that they are not getting much out of the lesson. Alternately, he or she may be very aware of students' emotional functioning but less attuned to their academic needs, not noticing when students do not appear to understand a concept. For example, the teacher may be teaching a lesson about the role of chlorophyll in determining leaf color and fail to notice that the students are not able to answer her questions or contribute to the lesson. She continues with the lesson for quite awhile before realizing that her students will require more background knowledge before they will be able to understand the chemical reactions to which she is referring. She does eventually respond by shifting to a more basic approach, which students respond to better. In the middle-range, the teacher may seem fairly aware of the needs of most students but may completely ignore a small percentage of students. This often can be observed when a teacher pays a lot of attention to students seated near him or in the front row but does not seem aware of students in the back and on the sides of the room or of events occurring in the back of the room.

The teacher is responsive to students sometimes but at other times is more dismissive or unresponsive, matching his or her support to the needs and abilities of some students but not others. This teacher may show elements of responsiveness but at times miss or ignore students' attempts to get his or her for attention and/or fail to elaborate on them. For example, during a book reading, the teacher may ignore several comments that a student makes such as, "I have a dog like that" and "We went on a trip, too!" The student clearly is excited to share this information, but the teacher fails to acknowledge the student's excitement and comments. At other times, the teacher may respond to the students' comments. For example, when two students show her their new shoes, she elaborates on how she likes their shoes and how she just bought new shoes, too. This teacher may allow emotional expression only at certain times or under certain circumstances—perhaps finding time to talk about positive events but not about negative feelings; for example, she may acknowledge a student's excitement over an upcoming party but respond negatively to a student who is visibly upset because he did not get a turn on the classroom computer. Instead of saying that she understands that he is disappointed but that perhaps he can sign up for the computer tomorrow, she makes a comment such as, "It's okay—it's no big deal." As another example, a teacher in this range may respond to students who actively and obviously seek him or her for assistance but not respond to more subtle behavioral cues that students need help, such as looking down or around the room or fidgeting with materials rather than fully engaging in an activity. This teacher may make efforts to individualize support to different students according to their needs but may not always be successful in matching his or her help to their skill levels. For example, the teacher may make a concerted effort to help a group that is struggling to complete a project, but once he has helped them get started, fail to stop and take a step back to see if they can begin to work more independently.

The teacher is sometimes effective at addressing students' problems and concerns. The teacher may make an effort to respond to students' needs and concerns, but these efforts may not always communicate genuine concern or successfully soothe the students. At times, the teacher may acknowledge a student's distress, but his or her approach to problem solving may be to minimize the concern as not being important and try to get the student to move on without having adequately processed the student's problem. This inconsistent sensitivity may result in some students having to approach the teacher several times with the same question or problem because it was not adequately addressed the first time. In some cases, the student may reengage in an activity but with signs that he or she does not feel heard and understood, such as displaying a glum or sulking expression. A teacher in this range may make a good effort to address student problems in a timely manner, but certain students may fall through the cracks as the teacher tries to juggle multiple situations in the classroom.

The students sometimes seek support from, share their ideas with, or respond to questions from the teacher. Some students in this classroom may actively share thoughts and ideas and seek out the teacher for support, whereas other—perhaps more shy—students may hesitate and seem uncomfortable approaching the teacher or answering questions in class. Students may volunteer to answer questions when they are sure of the answers and comfortable with the content; however, when questions or materials are more challenging, students may become quiet and not be willing to take the risk of talking in front of the teacher or their peers.

High Teacher Sensitivity (6, 7)

The teacher is consistently aware of students who need extra support, assistance, or attention. The teacher anticipates problems and plans accordingly. He or she is so well attuned to the students that he or she is able to predict when the students are going to have academic, social, or behavior problems. For example, as a teacher is introducing the idea of having a "calendar kid," she says, "I know everyone wants to be a calendar kid, so we are going to make sure that everyone has a turn. If you don't get picked today, I promise that you will get a chance before too long." Or, when introducing an activity that she knows will be difficult for many students, she may say, "This is going to be a tough one, but you can ask me questions, and I'll be here to help you if you are having a hard time." The teacher notices when students are struggling to understand a lesson, are disengaged, or appear sad or anxious. He or she notices when students are not engaged in a task or are struggling emotionally, regardless of whether a student is involved in a whole-group conversation at the time or independent seatwork. Even when working with a small group of students, the teacher indicates awareness of students' activities and needs in other parts of the classroom.

The teacher is consistently responsive to students and matches his or her support to their needs and abilities. The teacher responds quickly when students make a comment, ask a question, or send behavioral signals indicating a need for help or attention. The sensitive teacher responds to students in a soothing and understanding manner, providing appropriate comfort, assistance, reassurance, and acceptance. The teacher acknowledges students' feelings regardless of whether they are positive or negative. For example, if a student arrives in the morning and is upset that she left her lunch on the bus, the teacher first acknowledges the student's feelings by saying, "I know you are upset about your lunch." He then provides reassurance, saying, "Let's talk to Mrs. Jackson, the bus driver, and try to find your lunch; if we don't find it before lunchtime, we have some food here to share." The sensitive teacher demonstrates understanding and knowledge about individual students. During group discussions or activities, the teacher may direct an individualized question to a student who has not participated in the group. By the same token, he or she may allow students to skip a turn when they do not feel they have a response ready. The teacher clearly knows the students well enough to be able to take their perspective during interactions. He or she may even verbalize the student's perspective as a way of providing support. For example, a student is having a hard time making a scale balance to get an accurate weight during a science lab and looks very frustrated. The teacher recognizes that this is difficult for the student but that he is working hard on it, and says to the student, "You are working so hard on getting that to balance just right so you can know exactly how much the tape weighs. I can see that you are frustrated because you want it to be exactly balanced and it keeps being just a bit off. Would you like my help or do you want to keep working on it by yourself?" This statement indicates not only that the teacher is responding to the student's feelings but also that she is responding in a way that is sensitive to the student's potential desire to do things on her own. The highly sensitive teacher serves as a secure base for students in the classroom. When a student is sad because of problems at home, the teacher may comfort the student, saying, "I know things are hard for you right now. Do you want to sit by me during group time?" or, "Hey, I haven't gotten to hear about how your birthday was last week. Do you want to come visit me and have a chat during lunch?" The teacher may demonstrate his or her understanding verbally, in the way that he or she speaks to the students, as well as nonverbally through his or her actions. The teacher may move closer to an area of the room where students are having difficulty with a particular task, thereby making him- or herself available to the group. Alternately, he or she may give a student who had a difficult morning a pat on the back or shoulder, offering her support to that student.

The teacher is consistently effective at addressing students' problems and concerns.

The highly sensitive teacher appears to be very in tune with his or her students, meaning that he or she consistently is able to see what students need both academically and socially and provides support to them in a timely manner. The teacher is focused on the needs of the students, and this awareness allows him or her to address problems as they arise. Students appear to be helped after interactions with the highly sensitive teacher; this may be observed when students become happily engaged in an activity after the teacher has addressed their concerns. The students of a highly sensitive teacher do not need to repeatedly seek out the teacher's help because their problems have been addressed the first time.

The students appear comfortable seeking support from, sharing their ideas with, and responding freely to the teacher.

Students in this classroom clearly see the teacher as a source of support—he or she serves as a "secure base" for them. This means that students can participate fully and work comfortably and freely on their own and in groups; they know that they can go to the teacher if a problem arises and the teacher will effectively help them resolve their problem. This consistent pattern of responsiveness on the part of the teacher allows students to take emotional and academic risks in the classroom. This is observed in the classroom when students spontaneously share their ideas and make attempts to answer even the most difficult questions.

Regard for Student Perspectives

Captures the degree to which the teacher's interactions with students and classroom activities place an emphasis on students' interests, motivations, and points of view and encourage student responsibility and autonomy

	Low (1,2)	Mid (3,4,5)	High (6,7)
Flexibility and student focus • Shows flexibility • Incorporates students' ideas • Follows students' lead	The teacher is rigid, inflexible, and controlling in his or her plans and/or rarely goes along with students' ideas; most classroom activities are teacher-driven.	The teacher may follow the students' lead during some periods and be more controlling during others.	The teacher is flexible in his or her plans, goes along with students' ideas, and organizes instruction around students' interests.
Support for autonomy and leadership • Allows choice • Allows students to lead lessons • Gives students responsibility	The teacher does not support student autonomy and leadership.	The teacher sometimes provides support for student autonomy and leadership but at other times fails to do so.	The teacher provides consistent support for student autonomy and leadership.
Student expression • Encourages student talk • Elicits ideas and/or perspectives	There are few opportunities for student talk and expression.	There are periods during which there is a lot of student talk and expression but other times when teacher talk predominates.	There are many opportunities for student talk and expression.
Restriction of movement • Allows movement • Is not rigid	The teacher is highly controlling of students' movement and placement during activities.	The teacher is somewhat controlling of students' movement and placement during activities.	The students have freedom of movement and placement during activities.

Low Regard for Student Perspectives (1, 2)

The teacher is rigid, inflexible, and controlling in his or her plans and/or rarely goes along with students' ideas; most classroom activities are teacher-driven. The content and method of instruction in this classroom are largely based on the teacher's agenda. The teacher rigidly adheres to an agenda or controls activities at the expense of providing learning opportunities and maximizing students' interest in activities. For example, as a student is making a card for a pen pal and is drawing a picture of a snowman, the teacher walks over and says, "It is spring. What are you doing drawing a snowman? Tell your pen pal about the flowers that are coming up now." In general, the teacher does not allow students to contribute their ideas to an activity and often provides all of the information and direction. The teacher does not follow students' lead in activities. For example, as the class is discussing synonyms, a child gives an example of an antonym and asks what it is. Instead of acknowledging that the student is thinking about how words are related to each other and letting him know that his example is called an antonym, the teacher just says, "We aren't talking about that right now. I'll tell you what that is in tomorrow's lesson." Or, as a student is writing enthusiastically about her weekend during morning journal time, the teacher may come up and say, "Tell me about our field trip; write something about that," changing the direction of the student's work. Often, the teacher appears to rigidly adhere to lesson plans. For example, he or she may read a lesson script without paying attention to opportunities to veer from the lesson in a way that will better match the students' interests.

The teacher does not support student autonomy and leadership. The teacher rarely looks for opportunities to involve students in a meaningful, formative way within the classroom. Teachers at the low end of this scale rarely, if ever, provide activities or opportunities within lessons for students to assert their independence or follow up on student-initiated activities or ideas. Students rarely have choices between or within activities and must complete tasks in a very rigid way. For example, the teacher may ask the students to make thank-you cards for the music teacher; instead of simply having the students make their own cards or write a letter to the music teacher, the teacher gives them a piece of photocopied paper with a musical instrument and the words "thank you" on it to color in. During center time or lab time, this teacher may provide very specific instructions about how students are to work at the centers or stations. For example, the teacher may have a center set up for students to make bags for Valentine's Day cards. The teacher already has completed an example and wants all students to make their bag exactly like hers. Each student is instructed to cut out one red heart, one pink heart, and a strip of paper for their name (which should be written in black on the strip) and then glue the decorations to their bag in a prescribed order. As another example, lab stations may be set up with fill-in-the-blank style forms. Students are instructed to complete very circumscribed tasks, such as weighing four objects on the table in a specific order and then writing the weight down in a particular blank on the page. The teacher may control all materials very tightly so that students have to ask the teacher's permission every time they want to use something. Students are not given opportunities to lead lessons or activities or given classroom responsibilities such as watering plants, cleaning tables, passing out papers, and so forth.

There are few opportunities for student talk and expression. Activities and lessons designed by this teacher provide few opportunities for students to share their ideas. The teacher does not make an effort to have students express their ideas during whole-group, small-group, or individual work. The teacher appears disinterested in understanding how the students "see the world" and in getting them to express these thoughts. Teacher talk predominates in this classroom. During whole- or small-group instruction, the teacher goes through lessons without encouraging students to talk by asking questions or prompting them to share their thoughts and ideas.

The teacher is highly controlling of students' movement and placement during activities. Some activities require more teacher control than others (e.g., whole-group activities versus free choice time or hands-on experimentation); however, the teacher consistently exerts a high degree of control over student movement regardless of the activity. The teacher frequently reminds students that they must stay on their bottoms, sit criss-cross, have hands in laps, be quiet, or sit still, even when these restrictions do not appear necessary. Students may be required to sit in their seats or at their desks and be prohibited from talking to their peers throughout the observation.

Middle-Range Regard for Student Perspectives (3, 4, 5)

The teacher may follow the students' lead during some periods and be more controlling during others. The classroom may seem moderately teacher-regimented, but some consideration is given to students' choices and interests during the observation period. The teacher sometimes rigidly adheres to an agenda or plan at the expense of learning opportunities and students' interest in activities but at other times appears more flexible and goes with the flow of students' ideas. At times, students may be moved through activities and lessons following the teacher's plan rather than the students' interests and understanding. For example, the teacher may create a writing center, an art center, and a science center based on the students' expressed interest in caterpillars, but the students may be required to remain in their centers until the bell rings rather than be allowed to move freely from center to center upon completion of an activity. Or, after students are particularly inquisitive about and interested in a project they have completed in small groups on the properties of light, the teacher may say that they do not have time for all groups to do all of the experiments but that she will allow a few extra minutes for the students to go around the room to other groups' tables and see what the other groups found during their work. Or, a student may bring up an idea during a group lesson and, rather than either going with the students' idea or completely dismissing it, the teacher may tell the student that he will think about doing it another time.

The teacher sometimes provides support for student autonomy and leadership but at other times fails to do so. The teacher may sometimes appear to look for ways to maximize students' autonomy but at other times asks students to complete activities in very rigid ways. For example, a teacher in this range may provide hands-on activities for students in which they can work autonomously in small groups, such as setting up a science experiment in which students compare the weights of different objects and then write a report about whatever data they found most interesting from the activity. However, the teacher tells the students the order in which they must weigh the various objects and collects the groups' data reports to read aloud to the class herself. Often, the teacher is supportive of students' autonomy during free choice times or centers but is much more controlling during structured lessons. For example, during center time, the students are free to choose what they would like to do; however, during a lesson on rhyming, the students must fill in a worksheet in which they draw a line between words that rhyme rather than, for example, come up with two rhyming words on their own or write a style of poem with a rhyming pattern. The teacher often uses whole-group instruction; although he or she may ask occasionally for student input and provide roles for one or two students, most of the lesson is teacher-driven and students are simply asked to respond to questions rather than play a more formative role. Students occasionally are given roles or responsibilities in the classroom. For example, the teacher may direct attendance but allow a student to hold the pointer and lead the calendar activity. Conversely, the teacher may allow a student to count the number of students in attendance but writes the number on the attendance chart him- or herself.

There are periods during which there is a lot of student talk and expression but other times when teacher talk predominates. In this classroom, teacher talk predominates but students do participate and are allowed to share ideas at a minimal level or for short periods of time. At times, the teacher may appear somewhat interested in getting students to share their view of the world but, at other times, seems more concerned with simply giving them information. For example, while reading a book about a boy losing his mitten, the teacher solicits ideas from the students about how the boy must feel and whether the students ever have lost something and how they felt about it; however, the teacher then goes on to read the rest of the book with no opportunities for student input.

The teacher is somewhat controlling of students' movement and placement during activities. At times, the teacher requires students to be quiet and remain seated, but other times the students may move about freely. For example, while students are playing a math facts game in small groups, the teacher may insist that they stay seated the whole time even though being seated makes it harder for them to reach the dice and see the game board. The students are allowed, however, to talk freely to one another during the game. As another example, the teacher may repeatedly remind students that they need to sit on their bottoms during whole-group time, even when a student is simply sitting quietly on her knees instead, but then allow the students to move around as needed when they transition to small groups.

High Regard for Student Perspectives (6, 7)

The teacher is flexible in his or her plans, goes along with students' ideas, and organizes instruction around students' interests. The teacher appears to be constantly on the lookout for opportunities to involve students in a meaningful, formative way within the classroom. The teacher does not rigidly adhere to an agenda or plan at the expense of learning opportunities and students' interest in activities. Being flexible and going along with students' ideas does not distract from the lesson but allows the teacher to incorporate the students' interests and ideas into the lesson or learning goals. For example, the students may be talking about the snow outside, so the teacher incorporates their questions into their morning weather discussion—he may even forgo attendance or some other part of the morning circle plan to go outside or look outside and focus on the students' interest in the weather. As another example, the teacher may start a lesson about exploration in early America by asking the students what they know about how people explored the American frontier and what they think it might have been like to be an early settler. The teacher then follows the students' interests, pace, and signals during the lesson. The teacher does not adhere to a specific script or outline for teaching the lesson; he does have some key points that he wants to address, but he lets those points come up naturally in response to the students' questions, suggestions, and discussions. When the students are particularly interested in one aspect of the lesson, the teacher spends extra time discussing that aspect. The teacher also may plan new activities in response to students' interests. This may be difficult to see during one morning of observation; however, an observer might note that the teacher has told students that he will develop a new activity for the next day to continue with a particularly exciting topic or that the teacher continues a bit longer than planned with a lesson because students are so interested. The teacher also may have built student-choice times, such as free reading or free writing, into the schedule.

The teacher provides consistent support for student autonomy and leadership. The teacher makes appropriate decisions enabling students to be as independent as possible within a given activity. Even in a structured lesson, a teacher can provide opportunities for students to be autonomous and have choices. For example, the teacher may be instructing students on how to write an essay with an introductory paragraph, a body paragraph, and a conclusion. To maximize students' autonomy within the context of this structured lesson, the teacher lets students generate the topic of the essay that they are working on as a class example and provide the sentences that go within each paragraph. Students in this particular lesson are not given complete freedom to choose what they will be doing because that would run counter to the goals of the lesson; however, a considerable effort is made to allow them to feel as if they are actively contributing to the activity. In terms of providing opportunities for student leadership, this teacher often may break the class up into several smaller groups for "jigsaw" book discussions or science experiments. In "jigsaw" discussions, each small group elects a "discussion leader," "recorder," "presenter" and so forth so that each student in the group has a specific and meaningful role to play. During morning meeting time, this teacher may make a considerable effort to ensure that students are involved in administrative tasks. For example, the teacher may have a student lead the class in their morning routine, read the morning news, or go over the day's schedule. During other times, the teacher structures lessons in a way that allows more student initiation and choice. The teacher may set up a science experiment on reflection and refraction in which students are able to choose objects to put into water or other liquids, determine if the object in the liquid reflected or refracted the light, and write down their personal observations to share with the group at the end. The teacher also responds to student initiation and ideas. When students say they want to learn more about a country they are studying in social studies, the teacher obtains additional resources for them and allows interested students to gather more information about the country during reading time and free time and then share what they learned at the end of the day or during the next social studies lesson. When students are particularly interested in the food of the country they are studying, the teacher brings in ingredients to make a small snack that people in that country would enjoy and sets up a cooking station for students to visit after they have finished writing a report about that country. The teacher makes materials available and accessible to the students, and they are not required to ask the teacher to gain access to or use them. Students often lead activities. For example, students may lead a transition by thinking up creative ways to dismiss their peers from one activity to go to the next. In classrooms with older students, student-led portions of lessons may be observed, in which groups of students study a particular topic and then teach what they have learned to their peers. In addition, there may be evidence in this classroom that students have classroom jobs such as "line leader," "paper-passer-outer," or "custodian."

There are many opportunities for student talk and expression. Activities and lessons provide ample opportunities for students to talk and share their ideas. The teacher appears genuinely interested in understanding how the students see the world and in getting them to express these thoughts. In these classrooms, student talk may predominate or be equal to teacher talk. During center or free time, students talk openly with teachers and with one another. During more structured teaching activities, teachers encourage a balance of student and adult talk by asking questions and making sure that students are given opportunities to be part of the activity and to share their perspectives. For example, while reading a book about fall, students are given the opportunity to share their ideas about what fall is and how they know it is fall.

The students have freedom of movement and placement during activities. Although teachers should have clear behavioral expectations for students, teachers high on this scale set behavioral expectations that are in line with students' developmental needs and appropriate to the activity at hand. For example, students may be free to choose the spot where they sit on the carpet during circle time or may be allowed to talk and move around freely during group projects. The teacher may invite students to feel free to move to a place where they can see best during lessons; or if a student is wiggling around a bit or standing up instead of sitting in his chair but is not interfering with his or other students' learning or attention, the teacher allows this to happen. This should not be confused with chaos; the teacher who scores high on this scale should have clear expectations for student behavior but not rigidly adhere to behavioral guidelines at moments when it is not necessary.

CLASSROOM ORGANIZATION

Behavior Management

Encompasses the teacher's ability to provide clear behavioral expectations and use effective methods to prevent and redirect misbehavior

Productivity

Considers how well the teacher manages instructional time and routines and provides activities for students so that they have the opportunity to be involved in learning activities

Instructional Learning Formats

Focuses on the ways in which the teacher maximizes students' interest, engagement, and ability to learn from lessons and activities

Behavior Management[3]

Encompasses the teacher's ability to provide clear behavioral expectations and use effective methods to prevent and redirect misbehavior

	Low (1,2)	Mid (3,4,5)	High (6,7)[4]
Clear behavior expectations • Clear expectations • Consistency • Clarity of rules	Rules and expectations are absent, unclear, or inconsistently enforced.	Rules and expectations may be stated clearly but are inconsistently enforced.	Rules and expectations for behavior are clear and consistently enforced.
Proactive • Anticipates problem behavior or escalation • Low reactivity • Monitors	The teacher is reactive, and monitoring is absent or ineffective.	The teacher uses a mix of proactive and reactive responses; sometimes he or she monitors and reacts to early indicators of behavior problems but other times misses or ignores them.	The teacher is consistently proactive and monitors the classroom effectively to prevent problems from developing.
Redirection of misbehavior • Effective reduction of misbehavior • Attention to the positive • Uses subtle cues to redirect • Efficient redirection	Attempts to redirect misbehavior are ineffective; the teacher rarely focuses on positives or uses subtle cues. As a result, misbehavior continues and/or escalates and takes time away from learning.	Some of the teacher's attempts to redirect misbehavior are effective, particularly when the teacher focuses on positive behavior and uses subtle cues. As a result, there are few times when misbehavior continues, escalates, or takes time away from learning.	The teacher effectively redirects misbehavior by focusing on positives and making use of subtle cues. Behavior management does not take time away from learning.
Student behavior • Frequent compliance • Little aggression and defiance	There are frequent instances of misbehavior in the classroom.	There are periodic episodes of misbehavior in the classroom.	There are few, if any, instances of student misbehavior in the classroom.

BEHAVIOR MANAGEMENT

---

[3]Behavior Management is often defined very broadly to include strategies that teachers use to keep students engaged as a means of preventing misbehavior. The CLASS Behavior Management dimension focuses on the prevention of more active misbehavior; the teacher's use of strategies to engage students is captured in Instructional Learning Formats.

[4]At the high end of Behavior Management, evidence of some teacher behaviors such as proactive strategies and effective redirection may not be evident because behavior is so well managed. If there is no evidence of student misbehavior, it is assumed that effective behavioral strategies are in place and a classroom may score in the high range.

Low Behavior Management (1, 2)

Rules and expectations are absent, unclear, or inconsistently enforced. At the beginning of activities, the teacher typically fails to tell or remind the students of the behavioral expectations for the activity. The teacher may enforce classroom rules inconsistently, sometimes getting angry when students talk out of turn while other times allowing a great deal of chaos. Students in these classrooms have a hard time knowing what kinds of behavior are acceptable, and this confusion can lead to increased behavior problems. The adults in these classrooms may have very different behavioral expectations, leading to inconsistent communication about expectations and enforcement of rules.

The teacher is reactive, and monitoring is absent or ineffective. This teacher seems one step behind in the classroom, reacting to rather than preventing misbehavior. For example, the teacher may not anticipate that some materials may be distracting for some students. She may pass out musical instruments for a lesson without telling students to wait to play their instruments until everyone has an instrument and has been given instructions for the activity. When the students quickly begin playing the instruments loudly, talking loudly to other students about the instruments, asking to trade, and so forth, the teacher reacts to the misbehaviors by telling the students to stop or by taking all the instruments back and lecturing students on what they did wrong. In addition, the teacher may exhibit a lack of monitoring or an inability to monitor all areas of the classroom at once; she may focus on only one area of the classroom or one group of students and ignore behavior problems in other areas, allowing the behaviors in these unmonitored areas to escalate. Or, a teacher may sit at her desk or talk with other adults and not pay attention to what is going on in the classroom. The lack of monitoring and failure to address early stages of problems with behavior in the classroom allows preventable situations to escalate or misbehavior to continue.

Attempts to redirect misbehavior are ineffective; the teacher rarely focuses on positives or uses subtle cues. As a result, misbehavior continues and/or escalates and takes time away from learning. In this classroom, the teacher may only notice and comment on misbehavior rather than provide students with positive feedback for meeting expectations and displaying appropriate behavior. For example, the teacher may repeatedly say, "You are too loud," instead of pointing out appropriate behavior when it occurs such as, "Thank you, Susan, for using an inside voice," or, "Thank you, Sam, for settling down quietly so you can hear me." Because the teacher's statements are focused on misbehavior, they give students no information about how to moderate their behavior to conform to the teacher's wishes and thus are typically ineffective in changing behavior (e.g., students may not know how loud is too loud). The teacher rarely, if ever, uses more effective redirecting techniques, such as eye contact, slight touch, gesture, physical proximity, asking a question about the current activity, or saying the student's name. Ineffective methods of dealing with minor misbehavior are those that take significant time and/or do not lead to improved student behavior.

There are frequent instances of misbehavior in the classroom. The students often engage in inappropriate behavior such as ignoring the teacher's directions, bickering with each other or with the teacher, leaving the area they are supposed to be working in, using materials inappropriately, and so forth. It is important to note that observers should look for active misbehavior, not just disengagement, which is coded under other dimensions. The classroom that rates low in this dimension may appear quite chaotic or there may be an accumulation of small misbehaviors over the course of the observation. To be scored in the low range on the Behavior Management dimension, it is not necessary for the majority of students to be misbehaving. Rather, there may be a few students whose disruptions significantly interfere with the classroom environment (e.g., intentionally interrupting lessons with inappropriate comments, challenging the teacher in a hostile manner during lessons, refusing to participate in activities) or many students who are consistently engaged in low-level misbehavior (e.g., playing with materials or talking to peers when they are supposed to be listening to the teacher).

Middle-Range Behavior Management (3, 4, 5)

Rules and expectations may be stated clearly but are inconsistently enforced. At times, the rules and expectations appear to be stated clearly and the students appear to know the rules of the classroom; at other times, the rules are either unclear or inconsistently enforced. For example, the students may quickly stop their activity and look up when the teacher uses a predetermined signal (e.g., turning off the lights, clapping, starting to sing a specific song). At other times, however, the teacher may ask the students to raise their hands when they are ready to answer but then allows students to call out their answers for a while before again asserting a need for them to raise their hands. This type of inconsistency is included under the Behavior Management dimension if it causes a disruption in the classroom. At times, the students are able to meet expectations for behavior; but at other times, they engage in inappropriate behavior such as throwing toys, arguing over materials, or stepping on a peer's work. Alternately, a minority of students may engage in minor misbehavior such as not paying attention or talking to peers when they are supposed to be listening to the teacher, but most of the students are considered well-behaved over the course of the observation. Also included in the middle range of this dimension are cases in which the lead teacher appears to have fairly consistent rules but the students spend substantial time with assistants or parent helpers who enforce the rules less consistently, leading to more student misbehavior.

The teacher uses a mix of proactive and reactive responses; sometimes he or she monitors and reacts to early indicators of behavior problems but other times misses or ignores them. Sometimes the teacher takes steps to anticipate and prevent misbehavior but at other times is more reactive than proactive. For example, the teacher may set clear expectations during whole-group time—"Okay, kids, I need everyone to sit with their eyes up front and have their listening ears on for the next few minutes"—but be less proactive, therefore spending more time and energy correcting students' misbehaviors, during center time or hands-on activities. The teacher may anticipate and avoid setting up some situations in the classroom that may cause behavior problems but fail to identify other situations that might cause problems. For example, the teacher may make sure he has enough sets of measuring cups for each of four groups of students but fail to gather enough materials that need to be measured to go around, causing the students to argue over who gets to use the materials first. This teacher may appear aware of potential problems in one area of the classroom or with one group of students but less aware of what is happening in other areas. Alternately, he may monitor students' behavior closely at times, such as during a whole-group lesson, but monitor them less effectively at other times, such as when they transition to small-group activities or individual seatwork.

Some of the teacher's attempts to redirect misbehaviors are effective, particularly when the teacher focuses on positives and uses subtle cues. As a result, misbehavior rarely continues, escalates, or takes time away from learning. Generally, students are considered to be well-behaved in this classroom; however, there may be periodic episodes of misbehavior in the classroom. The strategies that the teacher employs are considered both proactive and successful as well as some reactive and less successful. At times, the teacher makes use of positive feedback to reinforce and continue desired behavior (e.g., "I can tell that Danny is ready because he is sitting quietly and his eyes are on me") but at other times uses less positive strategies such as calling out the names of students who are not ready (e.g., "Tanya, we are going to wait to get started until you are ready to join us"). The teacher may use a mix of telling students what not to do (e.g., "Don't run in the class," "Don't mix the colors," "Don't push in line") and using positive phrases (e.g., "We walk in the classroom," "We need to keep our colors separate," "We line up and wait patiently"). Sometimes, comments and feedback are focused only on stopping inappropriate behavior or pointing out misbehavior, causing the teacher to miss opportunities to provide feedback to students who are meeting expectations and, consequently, increase the likelihood of positive behavior. Sometimes, the teacher responds to minor misbehaviors effectively, using strategies such as eye contact, touch, gesture, close physical proximity, asking a question about the current activity, or using the student's name (e.g., "Now, Eric, let's move on to page 12"). These means of redirection are generally quick and effective. However, at other times, the teacher ignores these behaviors or uses less effective methods such as constant reminders to "stop talking" or vague comments such as "I need you to get with it." There may be long periods during which the teacher seems to be managing behavior effectively; however, there are a few times when student misbehavior takes substantial time away from what the teacher is trying to accomplish in a lesson or activity. Alternately, a teacher may frequently provide very brief reminders to students to get them back on task. Although these reminders do not take substantial time away from the activity or lead activities to end prematurely, they interfere with the flow of the lesson.

There are periodic episodes of misbehavior in the classroom. At times, the students are able to meet expectations for behavior; but at other times, they engage in inappropriate behavior such as arguing with the teacher or peers, talking during lessons, arguing over materials, or stepping on a peer's work. Alternately, there may be a minority of students who engage in minor misbehavior such as not paying attention or playing with materials that they are supposed to be working with, but most of the students are considered well-behaved over the course of the observation.

High Behavior Management (6, 7)

Rules and expectations for behavior are clear and consistently enforced. In this classroom, the rules and expectations are clearly stated (e.g., posted in the room in short, simple statements) and/or there is evidence that all members of the classroom community understand the rules and expectations. Adults in the classroom enforce these same rules in a consistent and predictable manner. Teachers in this range often communicate behavioral expectations very quickly at the beginning of a lesson, perhaps by saying, "We are going to be working together on these projects; it is important for you to listen to one another carefully and keep your hands to yourself as you work with your classmates. It's okay for you to talk, but I need you to keep your voices at an indoor level."

The teacher is consistently proactive and monitors the classroom effectively to prevent problems from developing. Effective behavior managers are characterized by their proactive versus reactive response to a variety of situations within the classroom. They always appear to be one step ahead of problems in the classroom, anticipating and preventing misbehavior. This teacher anticipates and avoids setting up situations in the classroom that may cause behavior problems. For example, rather than putting a pile of books or materials in the middle of the rug for 20 kindergarten students to come grab at once, she puts smaller numbers of books out on individual tables so that students do not have to push each other to get to the books or materials. Or, before she begins a lesson, she asks students to put all other materials away so that they will not be distracted. A teacher who manages the classroom well is aware of students in all areas of the classroom, even when working with an individual student or a small group, and takes action to stop off-task behavior or misbehavior before it escalates into a more serious problem. If the teacher is working with a small group of students, she will make sure to scan the rest of the classroom frequently or assign another adult to monitor the behavior of the other students in the class while she works with the small group. During individual work or center time, the teacher walks around the classroom to reinforce students' on-task behavior.

The teacher effectively redirects misbehavior by focusing on positives and making use of subtle cues. Behavior management does not take time away from learning. This teacher consistently uses positive feedback that increases the chances that desirable behavior will be repeated and undesirable behavior eliminated. She may individualize her praise to specific students and about specific behavior. For example, if several students are still talking when they should be quiet and ready to listen to the teacher, the teacher may call attention to a few other students who are sitting quietly and looking at her by saying, "Thank you, Cindy and Dequan, for sitting quietly at your desk. I can tell you are ready." The teacher uses positive phrases that indicate what the students should be doing rather than behaviors that are prohibited. For example, the teacher tells the students to walk in the classroom, listen respectfully as peers are talking, and share materials, rather than telling them not to run, not to be rude, and not to take materials from one another. The feedback and comments that the teacher uses focus on the positive and tend to increase the likelihood of appropriate behavior. Additional effective means of redirecting students that the teacher may use include, but are not limited to, eye contact, touch, gesture, close physical proximity, asking a question about the current activity, or using the student's name (e.g., "Now, Eric, ready to review that last chapter?"). These means of redirection are generally quick and effective and do not take time away from instruction. Teachers who use effective behavior management spend very little time actually managing behavior problems because they are able to prevent many problems before they begin. When problems do occur, the teacher typically knows an efficient way to deal with them. Furthermore, the teacher's effective redirections prevent minor misbehavior from escalating.

There are few, if any, instances of student misbehavior in the classroom. When good behavior management has been established in the classroom, many students conduct themselves in an appropriate manner without reminders about rules and expectations because an established structure for appropriate behavior already exists. At the high end of this dimension, there may be no observed instances of misbehavior. The important distinction here between misbehavior and inattention is that although some students may appear interested or engaged in classroom work, they also are not engaged in behavior that is disruptive to others.

Productivity[5]

Considers how well the teacher manages instructional time and routines and provides activities for students so that they have the opportunity to be involved in learning activities

	Low (1,2)	Mid (3,4,5)	High (6,7)
Maximizing learning time • Provision of activities • Choice when finished • Few disruptions[6] • Effective completion of managerial tasks • Pacing[7]	Few, if any, activities are provided for students, and an excessive amount of time is spent addressing disruptions and completing managerial tasks.	The teacher provides activities for the students most of the time, but some learning time is lost in dealing with disruptions and the completion of managerial tasks.	The teacher provides activities for the students and deals efficiently with disruptions and managerial tasks.
Routines • Students know what to do • Clear instructions • Little wandering	The classroom routines are unclear; most students do not know what is expected of them.	There is some evidence of classroom routines that allow everyone to know what is expected of them.	The classroom resembles a "well-oiled machine"; everybody knows what is expected of them and how to go about doing it.
Transitions • Brief • Explicit follow-through • Learning opportunities within	Transitions are too long, too frequent, and/or inefficient.	Transitions sometimes take too long or are too frequent and inefficient.	Transitions are quick and efficient.
Preparation • Materials ready and accessible • Knows lessons	The teacher does not have activities prepared and ready for the students.	The teacher is mostly prepared for activities but takes some time away from instruction to take care of last-minute preparations.	The teacher is fully prepared for activities and lessons.

---

[5]Productivity ratings should not consider the quality of instruction or student engagement, which are considered in other dimensions.

[6]Some interruptions to instructional time may be out of the teacher's control (e.g., fire drills). Regardless of the cause of lost instructional time, simply code students' observed exposure to instructional activities.

[7]Observers should be conservative in judgments about the pacing of activities because in most classrooms there is significant variability in the amount of time students need to process information and complete activities. Only in cases of very slow pacing, in which a majority of students are clearly spending significant time waiting during instruction, should pacing influence a Productivity score.

Low Productivity (1, 2)

Few, if any, activities are provided for students, and an excessive amount of time is spent addressing disruptions and completing managerial tasks. Classrooms at the low end of the Productivity dimension are characterized by many periods during which students have no academic tasks to do or activities in which to participate. Instead, students may spend a lot of time waiting for the teacher while he is involved in irrelevant conversation or completes managerial tasks. For example, another teacher may spontaneously stop by to ask a question about a meeting they have later and, rather than asking the other teacher to come back at a better time, the teacher stops what he is doing and talks to his colleague for several moments, disrupting the activity or lesson. Or, a student may make an irrelevant comment during a reading activity (e.g., "My mom is bringing in cupcakes tomorrow"). Rather than acknowledging the student's comment and following up with the student later, the teacher stops the activity to ask the student questions. In addition, although all teachers need to complete managerial tasks, teachers at the low end of the Productivity dimension allow these tasks to take a great deal of time away from students' exposure to instructional activities. For example, the teacher may have students wait without an activity while he does attendance paperwork and completes the lunch count. This lack of activities also may occur as students finish work early or are getting ready for a new activity or lesson. For example, after a language arts lesson, students are asked to work independently on individual writing projects; some students inevitably finish their assigned tasks before others. In a classroom low on the Productivity dimension, those who finish early are not given another activity to work on (e.g., illustrating their work, looking at books, helping peers by editing their work) but instead are left to wait as the rest of the class finishes. Students in classrooms that score low in the Productivity dimension also spend a lot of time waiting as a result of the pacing the teacher uses. For example, the teacher may pass out students' individualized spelling flash cards one at a time, taking an extraordinary amount of time in setting up an activity rather than maximizing the time available to the students for actually participating in the activity. As another example of low productivity, the teacher may take considerable time passing out to each student pieces of paper with different units of measurement written on them (i.e., millimeter, centimeter, decimeter, meter, kilometer) and pieces of tape during a measurement activity. The teacher then has the students line up with their paper and tape and take turns going to the front of the class to tape their unit of measurement onto a large poster board, in order of size. The whole class waits as each student struggles to tape his or her piece of paper on the poster board evenly and in the appropriate place while leaving enough space for all the other papers.

The classroom routines are unclear; most students do not know what is expected of them. Classrooms scoring low on the Productivity dimension lack a daily routine or sequence of activities, causing frequent and lengthy losses of instructional time. For example, the teacher may fail to give students sufficient information about a hands-on group activity they are doing, resulting in a great deal of student confusion and time wasted waiting for the teacher to get around to the different groups' tables to reexplain the activity.

Many students may wander around the room, sit raising their hands without being involved in the activity, or repeatedly approach the teacher with questions during an activity; or, the teacher may frequently interrupt an activity to give students more directions and different instructions. These repeated interruptions disrupt the flow of the activity and may generate even more student confusion.

Transitions are too long, too frequent, and/or inefficient. The efficiency with which transitions occur is an important indicator of a classroom's productivity. Teachers in classrooms scoring low on the Productivity dimension do not make transition plans and directions explicit to the students. Students in these classrooms may appear confused about whether they are supposed to end their current activity, where to put away or get materials, what area they are responsible for cleaning up, or what they are supposed to do after they have finished their current activity. In addition, the teacher does not facilitate or inconsistently facilitates the students' transition (e.g., helping the students put away materials, making sure students know where they are supposed to be next) and instead is caught up in his own preparations for the next activity. Alternately, the teacher may not be consistent in following through with helping students put materials away and/or end an activity; as a result, a great deal of time is spent in transitions.

The teacher does not have activities prepared and ready for the students. The teacher in this classroom often is caught up in last-minute preparations for the next activity as students arrive and/or as students finish an activity and make the transition into another. He or she may have to stop a lesson to go get needed materials or may seem to forget what it is he is trying to accomplish, having to refer frequently to directions or a script for the activity in a way that disrupts the progression of the learning experience.

Middle-Range Productivity (3, 4, 5)

The teacher provides activities for the students most of the time, but some learning time is lost in dealing with disruptions and the completion of managerial tasks. Classrooms scoring in the middle range for Productivity include certain periods in which clear activities are provided for students but other times during which students are predominately waiting for the teacher, wandering, or watching. For example, the teacher may have to interrupt a small-group lesson to find additional activities for students working in independent centers who have finished their activities. At times, the teacher allows disruptions to learning. For example, if another adult enters the room, the teacher stops his activity and talks with her instead of either having his assistant talk with the adult or asking the adult to come back in a few minutes. When students make irrelevant comments during activities, the teacher sometimes spends instructional time following up on the comments, thus getting the rest of the students off track. Although at times the teacher appears to accomplish managerial tasks efficiently, other times opportunities for learning are lost because of a lack of efficiency. For example, the teacher may have students wait for their name to be called to make their lunch choices, slowly read the entire class roster to take attendance, or check each student's backpack or folders for notes or money while the rest of the class waits. As another example, during an activity in which students have to guess how many items are in a series of jars, students may have to wait a long period of time between each guess as the teacher slowly writes the guess down. As yet another example, the teacher may ask one question and give all 18 students in the classroom an opportunity to respond individually, resulting in the other students having to sit and wait for a long period of time without having anything to do. The combination of these situations and/or the length of time that students spend simply waiting and not learning should help the observer determine the rating within the middle range.

There is some evidence of classroom routines that allow everyone to know what is expected of them. The teacher takes some steps to establish quick and effective routines but does not do so consistently. For example, instead of listing the possible activities to do following the completion of an activity or providing an overall schedule, the teacher may interrupt other lessons and activities to direct students about what to do next. In addition, the teacher's directions for activities may be somewhat vague, resulting in students spending some time asking the teacher what they are supposed to be doing or following a peer around. Once the teacher gives direction for centers, some students go to the centers and begin work as directed by the teacher, but other students look confused and get off-task when they get to the center or go to the wrong center altogether, requiring the teacher to take time away from the teacher-led group (causing those students to wait) to go help students who should be working independently. In other words, some students may appear to know the routine whereas others do not.

Transitions sometimes take too long or are too frequent and inefficient. The classroom may be quite productive during planned lessons and activities but fall apart during transitions from one activity to another. It is not always clear that the teacher has planned transitions or taken into account students' involvement in learning during transitions. During some transition periods, the teacher seems to take an intentional stance to structuring the students' time by, for example, providing clear and easy-to-follow directions for moving from center to center. Other transitions are less intentional. For example, there may not be a clear plan for how students should proceed from one activity to the next; therefore, students wait and wander around as they wait for more instructions or ask the teacher what they should be doing. Another example of an ineffective transition is when the teacher has the students rotate through centers extremely quickly (e.g., every 5–10 minutes). The students may be productively engaged when they are in the centers but, because of the quick turn around time, spend almost as much time getting from one center to another (e.g., cleaning up, walking to the other center, figuring out what they should do at the center) as they do productively engaged in activities.

The teacher is mostly prepared for activities but takes some time away from instruction to take care of last-minute preparations. This teacher appears to have put time into getting ready for activities ahead of time but still may not be fully prepared. For example, the teacher may have taken out a set of cards needed for an activity but when it comes time to use the cards has to spend quite a bit of time looking through the stack of cards to find the ones he needs. As another example, the teacher may have planned to have the students look at a set of objects and determine which objects are transparent and which are opaque; but although he has taken out all of the materials, he still has to look around for several minutes for the flashlight. These brief interruptions add up and take important time away from instruction.

High Productivity (6, 7)

The teacher provides activities for the students and deals efficiently with disruptions and managerial tasks. In this classroom, it would be difficult to imagine more instructional time being squeezed out of the day. Activities and centers are ready and available as soon as students arrive in the classroom, and the teacher has a clear plan for what the students can do. When students finish an activity early, there are clear choices for transition activities, such as reviewing spelling words or reading. The teacher does not allow disruptions to interfere with activities. Productive teachers are good at minimizing the number and length of disruptions to learning. For example, if an announcement comes on over the public address system, the teacher has the students listen but then quickly reengages them in the activity at hand. The teacher does not let irrelevant comments or questions lead away from the task at hand for long periods of time. For example, during a lesson on multiplication, a student may pick up an irrelevant detail in a word problem and focus on that. For example, in a problem asking how many oranges there are total if a group of 12 children each have 4 oranges, a student might call out, "I don't like oranges. I like apples better than oranges!" The productive teacher will respond briefly to this comment so the student knows she has been heard but then gets back to the lesson, such as by saying, "Hmmm, let's hope these kids like oranges, because how many will they have all together?" All teachers must deal with managerial tasks at times, but the highly productive teacher deals with these tasks in a way that minimizes the loss of instructional time. For example, if the teacher needs to check work, he first makes sure the students are involved in another activity or involves the whole group in checking work so that students are not waiting. As another example, to complete attendance, the teacher has the students estimate the number of boys and the number of girls and identify who is absent. As individual students give their estimates, the teacher asks the other students to determine whether they agree with those estimates or to compare today's estimates with yesterday's.

The classroom resembles a "well-oiled machine"; everybody knows what is expected of them and how to go about doing it. In highly productive classrooms, students and teachers go about the school day in an organized, efficient manner. Students know what they should be doing and how to get help if they need it. They can quickly locate needed materials in the room and easily follow teacher's instructions. The teacher provides clear instructions that are understood by all students. There are few, if any, instances in which students with the same problem or question about what to do repeatedly interrupt a teacher, and students rarely wander about aimlessly. A teacher who scores high on this dimension typically will include clear directions or options for students who finish their work early and provide an overall schedule to students so they know the agenda for the day or for a particular activity. For example, the teacher may tell the students that they will be working on handwriting as a whole group and, then will complete individual worksheets. Once they are done with their worksheets, they should take their book of the week out of their desks and read while they wait for the teacher to come give them feedback and for the rest of the class to finish. Alternatively, the teacher may have several centers available and ready for students, explain all of the centers beforehand, and have reminder cards posted at each table so that students can move independently from center to center as they finish work and not have to check in with the teacher about what to do next, thus preventing the students from wandering aimlessly around the classroom.

Transitions are quick and efficient. During transitions, the students know what is expected, do not need to be reengaged, and quickly move from activity to activity gathering or putting away necessary materials. Highly productive teachers maintain the focus of transitions by monitoring what students are doing to get ready for the next lesson instead of being distracted by trying to get their own materials together. Highly productive teachers also minimize the time spent in transition by giving clear directions such as, "Put these papers in your blue folders, open up your math books (which the teacher has already placed on students' desks), and turn to page 12," and helping students who appear to be struggling. The teacher may use transitions as learning opportunities by, for example, dismissing students to their centers based on what color or pattern they are wearing or by calling out a letter and telling students that they can move on the next activity if they have that letter in their name. Another productive transition strategy is to include the transition as part of the lesson. For example, during a lesson on gravity, the teacher may instruct the students to get up out of their seats and sit on the carpet while thinking about how gravity works with or against them as they perform this task. This strategy allows all students to be thinking and involved in the activity while they move from one area to another.

The teacher is fully prepared for activities and lessons. The highly productive teacher is clearly ready for all activities and lessons. Materials are ready and easily accessible, and the teacher clearly knows how to implement an activity without having to constantly look at directions or a script. If the teacher is reading word cards, it is clear that he or she has reviewed the words and pictures and is able to explain the pictures and words to the students without having to refer back to the lesson plan. If the students are getting ready to go to hands-on centers, the teacher has all materials already out on the tables or has a quick, easy way for students to get what they need. The teacher has enough of all of the ingredients and measuring tools and the directions are ready so that when students get to their lab table or center they can begin work right away. If students are going to a publishing center, paper, pencils, and illustrating materials are available when the students enter the center.

Instructional Learning Formats

Focuses on the ways in which the teacher maximizes students' interest, engagement, and ability to learn from lessons and activities

	Low (1,2)	Mid (3,4,5)	High (6,7)
Effective facilitation • Teacher involvement • Effective questioning • Expanding children's involvement	The teacher does not actively facilitate activities and lessons to encourage students' interest and expanded involvement.	At times, the teacher actively facilitates activities and lessons to encourage interest and expanded involvement but at other times merely provides activities for the students.	The teacher actively facilitates students' engagement in activities and lessons to encourage participation and expanded involvement.
Variety of modalities and materials • Range of auditory, visual, and movement opportunities • Interesting and creative materials • Hands-on opportunities	The teacher does not use a variety of modalities or materials to gain students' interest and participation during activities and lessons.	The teacher is inconsistent in his or her use of a variety of modalities and materials to gain students' interest and participation during activities and lessons.	The teacher uses a variety of modalities including auditory, visual, and movement and uses a variety of materials to effectively interest students and gain their participation during activities and lessons.
Student interest • Active participation • Listening • Focused attention	The students do not appear interested and/or involved in the lesson or activities.	Students may be engaged and/or interested for periods of time, but at other times their interest wanes and they are not involved in the activity or lesson.	Students are consistently interested and involved in activities and lessons.
Clarity of learning objectives • Advanced organizers • Summaries • Reorientation statements	The teacher makes no attempt or is unsuccessful at orienting and guiding students toward learning objectives.	The teacher orients students somewhat to learning objectives, or the learning objectives may be clear during some periods but less so during others.	The teacher effectively focuses students' attention toward learning objectives and/or the purpose of the lesson.

Low Instructional Learning Formats (1, 2)

The teacher does not actively facilitate activities and lessons to encourage students' interest and expanded involvement. At the low range of the Instructional Learning Formats dimension, the teacher makes few, if any, attempts to facilitate students' engagement in activities or lessons. For example, the teacher may give students an activity to complete, such as making visual representations of multiplication problems using unifix cubes or completing a math worksheet, but the teacher does not walk around the room, ask questions about students' progress, talk with students about decisions they are making, or offer additional information to assist students in participating in the activity. Or, the teacher may set up science lab tables with objects made of different materials for the students to explore the differences between objects in terms of properties such as weight, density, and texture; however, the teacher sits at the front of the classroom, passively monitoring the students and does not become involved in the activity or provide guidance for students' expanded participation. The teacher may not ask any questions to facilitate students' involvement or may ask so many questions (sometimes answering them herself) or participate so much that students are not able to take ownership or be maximally involved in the activity.

The teacher does not use a variety of modalities or materials to gain students' interest and participation during activities and lessons. The teacher relies on one presentation modality (e.g., listening) without attending to the other modalities (e.g., movement, vision, nonverbal expression and behavior) through which information can be communicated. Or, if a teacher does attempt to use other modalities, he or she is ineffective. For example, a teacher may use a dry erase board to write down students' ideas, but because her writing is so small or messy the communication value is minimal and her actions do not serve to increase students' involvement in the activity. Or, a teacher may have picture cards to go along with a book, but the cards are so small they serve as more of a distraction than a contribution to the students' involvement in the lesson. In addition, there is little or no evidence that the teacher has planned exciting, creative activities for the students using a variety of materials and different types of activities. The teacher does not provide hands-on materials. The teacher controls the materials or relies on lecture or worksheets.

The students do not appear interested and/or involved in the lessons or activities. The students generally do not volunteer, raise their hands, or participate in the activity or lessons presented by the teacher. Instead, they appear bored or disengaged. The teacher does not make efforts to facilitate students' attention to the activities or lessons and, as a result, the students do not actively participate or expand their involvement in the activity. During independent centers or seatwork, for example, the teacher often sits at her desk, removed from the students. Even if she is physically near them, she does not make an effort to facilitate their participation. As a result, a large group of students are not interested or engaged in the activities and some may be wandering around or merely watching peers work.

The teacher makes no attempt or is unsuccessful at orienting and guiding students toward learning objectives. Students in this classroom appear unaware of how they should be focusing their attention in the lesson or activity. The teacher fails to use strategies such as *advanced organizers* (e.g., "Okay, let's think about which objects are heavier; hold a ball and a rock and think about which one feels heavier to you"), *summaries* (e.g., "So we just talked about how different objects have different weights or feel heavier than other things"), and *reorientation statements* (e.g., "We are getting a bit off track; let's make sure we are thinking about how these things are heavier or lighter than other objects, not just about their shape and size") to draw students' attention to learning objectives. The teacher in the classroom that scores low on the Instructional Learning Formats dimension may seem to ask a series of unrelated questions that confuse students rather than keep his or her questioning and directions clear and targeted on the learning objective. It often seems unlikely that students could identify the learning objectives or activity in which they are involved.

Middle-Range Instructional Learning Formats (3, 4, 5)

At times, the teacher actively facilitates activities and lessons to encourage interest and expanded involvement but at other times merely provides activities for the students. The teacher makes some attempts to actively engage students in seat or center work by moving around the classroom, asking questions, getting involved in activities, working with the students, and so forth; at other times, however, he or she passively monitors students' activities and does not offer opportunities for expanded learning through questioning or involvement. During whole-group instruction, the teacher sometimes works to actively engage students by asking questions to involve students in the activity but at other times merely presents information to the students. During centers or lab time, the teacher sometimes goes around to the students' different activities and participates as an active member, asking about where they are in the activity, what they are doing, and what they are learning; but at other times, he or she is not attentive to their activity. The teacher in this range also occasionally may become overinvolved in the activity, asking too many questions of students, answering his or her own questions, or not allowing students to explore. Many other times, the teacher facilitates the activity with some questions and allows appropriate time for students to explore independently.

The teacher is inconsistent in his or her use of a variety of modalities and materials to gain students' interest and participation during activities and lessons. The teacher may sometimes present information through a variety of modalities including vision, hearing, and movement to address students' different learning styles and attention, such as writing a large, clear list of what points students are bringing up during group brainstorming or reviewing discussions; however, he or she predominantly relies on one modality—often auditory presentation. The teacher appears to have put some thought into creating activities and structuring lessons so that students can actively explore and use materials to facilitate learning, but he or she is not always consistent in doing so. The teacher may come up with hands-on activities to follow a lecture or group discussion. For example, after talking about homophones and coming up with a list of different homophones as a group, the teacher may have a Homophone Memory game for students to play, in which they match different homophones in small groups or pairs. However, at other times, the teacher may just continue with a lecture format followed by worksheets. At times, hands-on opportunities are included in lessons. For example, the teacher may present the idea of force to the class in a science lesson and then have the students stand up and see how much force it takes to move different objects around the room. At other times, however, the teacher controls the materials and relies on lecture or worksheets. For example, during a science experiment involving adding food color to water, the teacher conducts all of the steps of the activity herself and does not let the students add drops of food coloring to the water or shake the bottle.

Students may be engaged and/or interested for periods of time, but at other times their interest wanes and they are not involved in the activity or lesson. As a result of the teacher's inconsistent facilitation of instruction, students in one center may appear engaged in an activity or lesson whereas students at another center are not. This may be observed when several students volunteer to answer questions or provide opinions and are called on by the teacher. These select students animatedly engage in a discussion and are clearly interested, but other students in the class who do not volunteer appear less interested. The middle-range teacher may miss opportunities to engage those students who do not volunteer to participate on their own.

The teacher orients students somewhat to learning objectives, or the learning objectives may be clear during some periods but less so during others. Students in this classroom sometimes appear aware of the point of lessons or how they should be focusing their attention but at other times seem unfocused on or unclear about the learning objectives. Or, one group of students working with the teacher may be clearly oriented to the lesson at hand whereas other students who are not working with the teacher are not. The teacher occasionally may use strategies such as *advanced organizers* (e.g., "Okay, let's take a picture walk through this book before we read it so we know something about what it will be about"), *summaries* (e.g., "So, we read about some different kinds of jobs people in the community have"), and *reorientation statements* (e.g., "We are getting a bit off track; let's make sure we are thinking about what kinds of jobs people you know might have, not just about people you know") to draw students' attention to learning objectives but other times fails to do so. The teacher sometimes asks a series of unrelated questions that confuse students but other times keeps her questioning and directions clear and focused on the learning objective. Sometimes the students in this classroom may be able to tell the observer what it was they were learning in a coherent way, but other times they may not.

High Instructional Learning Formats (6, 7)

The teacher actively facilitates students' engagement in activities and lessons to encourage participation and expanded involvement. During centers and seat work, the teacher moves around the room asking students questions, gauging their level of participation and their progress, participating in their activities, and so forth. His or her participation in the activities allows students to get the most out of the activities and materials that are available. During whole-group instruction, the teacher does not merely go through the motions of asking questions or answering them him- or herself; rather, he or she facilitates students' involvement through open-ended and factual questions that allow students to get involved in the activity or lesson and assist in their understanding. The teacher balances his or her involvement with student exploration to maximize students' participation and involvement. It should be recognized that teachers cannot be everywhere in the classroom and may not interact with every student during an observation period. However, classrooms can be rated at the high end of the Instructional Learning Formats dimension even if students do not have direct interactions with the teacher during the observation as long as the teacher has made an effort to distribute his or her attention across the class and facilitate as many students' involvement as possible. For example, during a science lab, the teacher may move around to check in on the different areas in the room. He may pause and help students assess whether their scale is balanced, asking questions about how much an object weighs and how that compares with how much they predicted that it would weigh, then move on to the next group of students and spend some time facilitating and participating in their efforts to compare the weight of one object to another, and finally check in with a third group of students, helping them resolve a discrepancy between the answers that two students have written down. This participation serves to enhance each group of students' involvement in the activities.

The teacher uses a variety of modalities including auditory, visual, and movement and uses a variety of materials to effectively interest students and gain their participation during activities and lessons. The teacher appears to be aware that to engage students most effectively he or she needs to use many different modalities; therefore, he or she presents information in a variety of ways with a variety of materials. For example, the teacher may read the students a book and give each of the students a felt picture that corresponds to some event in the story. When the teacher reads about each event, the student with that felt piece gets to come up and put it on the felt board. As another example, during a lesson on place words (e.g., *next to, between, beside*), the teacher asks students to get up and move somewhere in the room (e.g., "Go stand next to the blocks") and then tell her where they are standing. In addition, the teacher makes an effort to provide interesting hands-on opportunities for students using exciting materials. For example, after students read about different countries in social studies, they may get together with other students who have learned about the same country and write a summary of what they have learned. Then, they might build a three-dimensional map of the country out of clay and have the opportunity to paint the map to reflect major topographical features of the country. During major transition times and break time, the teacher may play music from the different countries that the class is studying. The teacher makes an effort to create a hands-on component to each unit or lesson. During the demonstration of a volcano, students get to pour the vinegar, the liquid that causes the volcano to erupt. During a lesson on volume, students get to drop 1 ml of water into a liter jar to compare the relative amounts of liquid. The teacher makes limited use of lectures and presentations in which there is no student participation. However, the teacher may maximize students' learning without the use of manipulatives or hands-on exploration if she is effectively engaging students using other methods, such as effective questioning, comparisons, and examples. When the teacher uses these strategies successfully, students will display very high levels of engagement and their learning is maximized.

Students are consistently interested and involved in activities and lessons. Students listen to the teacher, raise their hands or volunteer information, respond when asked direct questions, and actively participate in whole-group lessons, centers, or seat work. During playtime, the students are full participants in the pretend-play process, in making up stories, in talking with peers, in asking adults to come to their restaurant or store, and so forth. During the lecture-based portion of the lessons, students are clearly interested in what the teacher has to say, sharing their knowledge, offering their opinions at appropriate times, and responding to teacher prompts for them to think about and respond to the material being presented. They appear enthusiastic about moving on to do independent follow-up work or seatwork after the teacher has finished with the class discussion aspect of the lesson. During hands-on portions of lessons, students actively and enthusiastically manipulate materials and make full use of the materials that the teacher has provided for them. For example, during an activity in which students are given various musical instruments, the vast majority of students play the instruments and explore the sounds that the different instruments make. When students work with partners using popsicle sticks to represent the relevant numbers in multiplication word problems, they fully participate in the activity, work animatedly with their partners, discuss how many groups of sticks they need and how many sticks in each group, and get excited about visually representing their problem and then working out the solution rather than just playing with the sticks distractedly.

The teacher effectively focuses students' attention toward learning objectives and/or purpose of the lesson. Students in this classroom appear aware of the point of lessons or how they should be focusing their attention during activities. The teacher frequently uses strategies such as *advanced organizers* (e.g., "Okay, let's take a picture walk through the book before we read it so we know something about what it will be about"), *summaries* (e.g., "So we just talked about occupations people might have and the different responsibilities that go along with each one"), and *reorientation statements* (e.g., "We are getting a bit off track; lets make sure we are thinking about what responsibilities you think the different jobs would include—not just listing the jobs") to draw students' attention to learning objectives. During both whole group and center activities, the teacher keeps his or her questioning and directions clear and targeted on the learning objective. During centers, the teacher focuses his or her questions on the activity in which the students are involved. For example, when students are having a book discussion, the teacher prompts them to consider different aspects of the book, such as the main characters, the plot, and the central conflict, and asks them how they think the book will end. (If the students' attention to the activity begins to wane, the effective facilitator will pick up on this and change the line of questioning or have the students start to ask questions of one another in order to reengage the class.) Students in this classroom should be able to tell the observer in a coherent way what it was they were learning.

INSTRUCTIONAL SUPPORT

Concept Development

Measures the teacher's use of instructional discussions and activities to promote students' higher-order thinking skills and cognition and the teacher's focus on understanding rather than on rote instruction

Quality of Feedback

Assesses the degree to which the teacher provides feedback that expands learning and understanding and encourages continued participation

Language Modeling

Captures the quality and amount of the teacher's use of language-stimulation and language-facilitation techniques

Concept Development[8]

Measures the teacher's use of instructional discussions and activities to promote students' higher-order thinking skills and cognition and the teacher's focus on understanding rather than on rote instruction

	Low (1,2)	Mid (3,4,5)	High (6,7)
Analysis and reasoning • *Why* and/or *how* questions • Problem solving • Prediction/experimentation • Classification/comparison • Evaluation	The teacher rarely uses discussions and activities that encourage analysis and reasoning.	The teacher occasionally uses discussions and activities that encourage analysis and reasoning.	The teacher often uses discussions and activities that encourage analysis and reasoning.
Creating • Brainstorming • Planning • Producing	The teacher rarely provides opportunities for students to be creative and/or generate their own ideas and products.	The teacher sometimes provides opportunities for students to be creative and/or generate their own ideas and products.	The teacher often provides opportunities for students to be creative and/or generate their own ideas and products.
Integration • Connects concepts • Integrates with previous knowledge	Concepts and activities are presented independent of one another, and students are not asked to apply previous learning.	The teacher sometimes links concepts and activities to one another and to previous learning.	The teacher consistently links concepts and activities to one another and to previous learning.
Connections to the real world • Real-world applications • Related to students' lives	The teacher does not relate concepts to the students' actual lives.	The teacher makes some attempts to relate concepts to the students' actual lives.	The teacher consistently relates concepts to the students' actual lives.

CONCEPT DEVELOPMENT

---

[8]The Concept Development dimension is not just about the development of a specific concept (e.g., seasons, subtraction) but about teachers' use of strategies to encourage understanding and thinking skills.

Low Concept Development (1, 2)

The teacher rarely uses discussions and activities that encourage analysis and reasoning. In this classroom, the teacher makes no attempt to develop students' understanding of ideas and concepts; the preponderance of teaching is focused only on getting students to remember and repeat facts and practice basic skills. Alternately, there may be no instructional opportunities provided. Teachable moments that could develop students' thinking are missed as the teacher moves through the activity focusing on facts, recall, and repetition—not on the process of learning or exploration. Students are frequently engaged in completing basic drill-oriented worksheets or activities that generally have one correct way to be done, and the teacher's goal for the activity is correctness or completeness. During a book reading, the teacher focuses on facts in a traditional recall format, asking students questions such as, "What animal was this book about?" "What was the main character's name?" or "What letter does the word *lion* start with?" The teacher does not solicit ideas focused on analysis and reasoning from the students, such as asking why something may have happened in the book or what might happen next. Instead, the teacher is solely focused on the students' ability to recall facts from the book. During the morning meeting, the teacher may ask the students whether it is raining but does not elaborate about what happens when it rains or what you might need to wear if it is raining—he merely is asking for a yes or no response. He may ask students how many more boys than girls are in the class or what day comes after Monday, but he does not ask these questions in the context of a discussion in which he expects the answers to be anything more than rote. The teacher does not ask students to engage in problem solving and does not use strategies such as prediction, experimentation, comparisons, classifications, and so forth. For example, during a lesson on shapes, the teacher holds up a hexagon and asks students to name it, then holds up a rhombus and asks them to do the same. The teacher is focused on getting students to recall information rather than drawing their attention to ways to classify or compare shapes (e.g., straight versus curved lines, number of sides and vertices). As another example, while reading a book about homesteaders during the western expansion of the United States, the teacher only asks fact recall questions about what new states were settled; he does not ask questions about the similarities and differences among people who opted to become homesteaders, what students predict would have changed for people when they moved to the frontier, or why people might have decided to move west to farm the land. The teacher does not ask students to engage in any evaluation of their own and misses opportunities to let students think about summarizing their ideas and work. Instead, the teacher may move quickly from one activity to another without giving students a chance to think about what they just completed.

The teacher rarely provides opportunities for students to be creative and/or generate their own ideas and products. The focus in this classroom is on having students complete activities and provide correct answers rather than on helping to stimulate their creativity and ability to plan. The teacher fails to make use of brainstorming as a way to get students thinking. For example, after reading an essay, the teacher asks questions such as, "Why did the author say she moved?" with the explicit goal of having students recall a fact from the story. Instead, the teacher could have asked, "What was going on during this time in our history that would have made some people want to move?" allowing students to think of many possible responses. Or, if a student is working on a writing project and asks the teacher for help, rather than helping the student think about the different ways she might organize her writing and how setting, characters, and plot might come together to make a good story, the teacher simply tells the student what to write about. The teacher also places no emphasis on helping students generate plans about how they will spend their time or how they will go about a particular task. For example, as students are beginning work on a project building something out of three-dimensional shapes, the teacher does not ask them to think about what they want their final project to look like and how they are going to pick different three-dimensional shapes and put them together to build their final project; rather, he tells them to make sure that they have used all the shapes and that their finished project looks like a house or a building.

Concepts and activities are presented independent of one another, and students are not asked to apply previous learning. In this classroom, the teacher moves from one distinct subject to another and makes no attempts to link concepts. Activities and lessons are not designed in a way that encourage making connections between concepts. For example, when going over the circle-square pattern she has created on the calendar, the teacher does not link the patterning back to the patterns the students created using cardboard circles and squares earlier in the day. Or, after the students have read a book about spring, the teacher does not make the connection between the planting that happened in the book and the seeds that the class planted in their window boxes outside. In centers, the teacher makes no attempt to talk with the students about integrative concepts or provide activities that help students integrate knowledge. The teacher also fails to help students make links between new concepts and things they have previously learned. The teacher does not ask questions to help in understanding what students may already know about a subject but simply presents new information as distinct from any previous knowledge.

The teacher does not relate concepts to the students' actual lives. Activities and instruction in this classroom seem abstract and removed from the students' everyday lives. The teacher does not provide opportunities for the students to apply knowledge to meaningful activities. For example, a teacher may conduct a lesson on the letter *t* but focus only on what a *t* looks like and how it sounds. He may make no attempts to have students look around the classroom for items that begin with *t*, generate a list of their own words that start with *t*, or think of everyone in the room who has a *t* in their name. Or, the teacher may be engaged in a lesson on the sense of hearing and simply talk about hearing rather than provide students with an activity that allows them to experience and understand the idea of hearing. The teacher also fails to use strategies that help students relate abstract ideas to their own lives. For example, during a lesson on sharing, the teacher may talk about why it is good to share but not ask the students questions about whether they share in the classroom or at home or, if they do share, how it makes them feel and why. The focus of the lesson appears to be on relaying information rather than making that information meaningful to the students. The teacher also may present information or ideas that seem very abstract to most students without making attempts to make them more meaningful. For example, a teacher may read a passage that defines the concept of *work* (i.e., applying a force that moves an object) in science but not talk with students about how they may do this kind of work in their everyday lives. Which things that the students think of as work would or would not count as work in science? In other words, the teacher does not ask questions such as, "Does it feel like work when you are sitting still reading a page in your book for homework? But is that work in science?"

Middle-Range Concept Development (3, 4, 5)

The teacher occasionally uses discussions and activities that encourage analysis and reasoning. Opportunities for analysis and reasoning are interspersed with more rote types of learning. When the teacher does focus on the meaningful understanding of ideas, the discussion is usually brief and returns to more fact-based instruction. Or, the teacher seems to occasionally ask questions that require higher-order thinking skills, but these questions seem isolated rather than consistently and intentionally crafted to expand students' thinking. The teacher sometimes asks why and how questions but other times fails to provide opportunities to help students engage in analysis or reasoning. During a book reading, the teacher may initially ask a few open-ended questions, such as, "How do you think the girl feels, being so much taller than her friends?" or "What could the girl do when someone teases her?" After these initial questions, however, the teacher often resorts to more test-like questions that have one correct answer or are easily answered, such as, "What do you see on this page?" or "What was her brother's name?" The teacher may present some activities or questions that allow students to solve problems. For example, the teacher may ask students to predict how many tennis balls they can fit into a container or to think about what else could have happened in a story. More often, however, the teacher asks questions that require only a one-word answer from students, have only one possible correct answer, and focus more on repetition as opposed to stimulating thinking or learning processes. When a teacher does use strategies that encourage analysis and reasoning, they typically are not extended instructional discussions and, therefore, students' opportunities to engage in this higher-order thinking is not maximized. Occasional opportunities may exist for students to compare and contrast ideas, materials, and so forth. For example, the teacher may set up a science lab in which small groups of students categorize objects that are similar by weight, density, or volume. Once each group is finished categorizing their objects, the students in the other groups have to try to determine what the categorizing factor was by looking at how the objects are grouped. Despite taking the time to set up this interesting lab, the teacher does not walk around facilitating the activity; and when the activity is finished, the teacher resorts to a more rote style of fact-based questioning instead of asking students how they figured out what each group was using to categorize their materials. As a result, some students in the class are really thinking about classification schemes, whereas others are simply guessing based on extraneous factors and never are asked to explain or justify their reasoning. The teacher occasionally asks students to engage in an evaluation of their own work or summarize ideas and work, but these are brief rather than sustained efforts. For example, the teacher may ask students to tell him briefly what they are learned from an activity but then move on without further comment or conversation.

The teacher sometimes provides opportunities for students to be creative and/or generate their own ideas and products. These opportunities do not appear to be intentionally organized by the teacher or they happen only occasionally. For example, the teacher may have students engage in a short brainstorming task at the start of a lesson but then quickly moves on to a more rote activity. Or, as the teacher interacts with students during center time, he may ask occasional questions that encourage the students to generate ideas and plan, but these interactions are not frequent.

The teacher sometimes links concepts and activities to one another and to previous learning. The teacher makes some attempt to integrate ideas across the curriculum, but these attempts are typically brief. For example, while reading a book about cars, the teacher may say, "Yesterday we talked about plane shapes. What plane shapes do you see on this page?" Once the students respond, however, he may move on with the story rather than talk more extensively about how you can see plane shapes in many everyday things. The teacher seems to mention connections and integrations in passing rather than design activities specifically to help students connect different concepts. The teacher may occasionally ask students to make inferences from what they already know or ask them to tell him about their previous knowledge.

The teacher makes some attempts to relate concepts to the students' actual lives. Although this teacher makes comments and asks questions that help relate concepts to students' lives, he fails to elaborate on them in a way that makes the connection concrete for many students. For example, when teaching students about prepositions, the teacher may ask one or two questions related to how students use these words in everyday life, such as, "When might we need to use prepositions when we are talking with our friends or our family? How about if you are telling someone how to find something?" However, the teacher does not ask the students to think about and share examples of times they have recently used a preposition to help someone locate something or explain an object's position in time or space. As another example, when talking about the community and people's jobs, the teacher may ask students about their parents' jobs but not further the discussion by asking about other jobs in the community, such as those at the post office, grocery store, or bank.

High Concept Development (6, 7)

Note: For the high range of the Concept Development dimension, the teacher provides the following types of learning opportunities to most of the students; however, it is possible to score at the high end without a teacher having interactions with all students during a single observation period. For example, during center time, there should be clear evidence that the teacher is engaging in these types of interactions with students as he moves around the classroom with the assumption that, over time, most students will be exposed to the interactions. During small- or whole-group time, the teacher should make attempts to interact with multiple students and provide instructional opportunities in such a way that the whole group is exposed to discussions.

The teacher often uses discussions and activities that encourage analysis and reasoning. This teacher consistently uses strategies that get students thinking about the how and why of learning rather than simply encouraging memorization of isolated facts. Although the teacher may ask some test-like and yes/no questions, the preponderance of the questions asked and activities provided are open-ended and facilitate students' use of analysis and reasoning. For example, while reading a book about animal training, the teacher asks questions such as, "Why do you think the man did just a little bit with each animal every day?" and "Do you really think that a dog could learn to bark in a way that sounds like he is saying words?" These initial open-ended questions lead to longer discussions in which the focus is on helping students gain a deeper understanding of concepts and develop thinking skills. Teachers can promote analysis and reasoning skills by focusing on *problem solving* (e.g., simulating a peer argument using puppets and talking with students about strategies the puppets could use and options they have), *experimentation and prediction* (e.g., the teacher may have an object in a bag and ask a student to try to guess what the object is based on clues that either the teacher or other classmates provide), *comparison and classification* (e.g., the teacher asks students to classify different kinds of trees according to whether they are evergreen or deciduous or has students categorize objects according to whether they are opaque, translucent, or transparent), and *evaluation/summarizing* (e.g., the teacher asks students to report on how well they think a particular activity went and why or asks a student to summarize what a passage was about). These are not isolated questions or activities but represent sustained opportunities for students to develop analysis and reasoning skills. In classrooms that score in the high range on the Concept Development dimension, teachers actively create opportunities for students to expand their analysis and reasoning skills by asking questions or otherwise encouraging students to use analysis and reasoning in their activities. For example, the teacher may point out an ambiguous illustration accompanying the text that the class is reading and ask the students, "What do you think they are trying to represent in this picture." This question is not intended to elicit one correct answer from students but rather to encourage them to use their reasoning skills to think about what the picture could be about given the subject of the text. The teacher accepts multiple answers to his question and does not focus on whether these are right or wrong; rather, he has each student provide their reasons for choosing the response that they did (e.g., "What about the picture makes you think it is showing the family leaving their home? I see what you mean. Caleb has a different idea; What does it look like to you Caleb? So you think it could be the family looking out at the plain and thinking what a big job they have ahead of them? What would you be thinking if that were you? Why?") During hands-on activities, teachers at the high end of the Concept Development scale do not simply give a task to students and walk away; instead, they stay with the students and encourage them to talk and think about the process of their activity by asking questions or pushing them to experiment in different ways. For example, working with a group of students during a lab on the reflective and refractive properties of light helps them get the most out of the activity by asking questions such as, "I see you have written down that the mirror reflects light. How did you figure that out? Is it the same if you put the mirror behind the cloth and shine the light on it through there?" or "Now, what if you look from this angle? Is it the same? How come? What happened?" In this example, the students may work independently, but they are given a framework for experimenting and exploring during the activity rather than just taking a quick look at an object and writing down "reflects" or "refracts." At the high end of this dimension, a teacher makes sure that students have time to respond when he asks questions.

The teacher often provides opportunities for students to be creative and/or generate their own ideas and products. The classroom provides many opportunities to stimulate students' creativity and ability to generate new ideas. The teacher often makes use of brainstorming as a way to get students thinking. For example, the teacher may ask questions such as, "What might we do to make sure that everyone gets a turn?" or "What kinds of materials will we need to make our gingerbread houses?" These types of questions allow students to think of many possible responses. Or, as part of the language arts curriculum, the teacher may have a publishing center where students come up with their own creative writing ideas, write down their "writer's plan," and then draft and edit their own novels or short stories. The focus in this center is on getting students to be creative, generate their own ideas, and come up with a product that reflects both their understanding of the writing process and their own unique stories. The teacher also may have a lab in which students can choose from a variety of materials to, for example, make a car that has the least friction and therefore can go the fastest. The teacher encourages students to try materials with different shapes, textures, and sizes to figure out which ones have the least friction. The teacher also places an emphasis on helping students generate plans about how they will spend their time or how they will go about a particular task by asking questions such as, "What will you start on?" "How will you keep track of what you have tried so far and what you thought about it?" or "Tell me how you are going to work together on this; what job will each person in your group have?"

The teacher consistently links concepts and activities to one another and to previous learning. The teacher makes an active effort to link together different concepts that the students have been studying or ties together multiple concepts within a single lesson. For example, when introducing a lesson on snow, the teacher may first talk with students about the other types of weather they have discussed. Then, as he talks more about snow, he makes consistent links back to previous weather discussions by asking questions such as, "How is snow different from rain?" The teacher also may ask students to apply previously learned knowledge to a current concept or problem. For example, he may be reading a story in which a society of two different varieties of aliens each think they are better than the other and have to learn to work together and respect each other for both groups to survive. The teacher asks students what this story makes them think about and facilitates students' tying this together with what they have been learning in history about our society and what they have been working on in terms of character development and interpersonal relationships within the classroom. The students may then work on writing their own stories on this general topic during language arts, and the teacher may present a science lesson on symbiotic organisms. At the high end of the Concept Development dimension, the teacher makes explicit attempts to tie together concepts in this way rather than simply mentioning connections in passing or on one isolated occasion. The teacher also embeds questions in the discussion that help him understand what students may already know about a subject, which then helps him best integrate their existing knowledge with new concepts.

The teacher consistently relates concepts to the students' actual lives. The teacher makes consistent and intentional efforts to make learning meaningful by helping students apply their thinking to real-world events and by covering concepts and ideas that are a part of students' everyday experience. For example, during a discussion of the sense of hearing, the teacher may first share, as an example, about how the crunching sound of stepping on leaves always reminds him of taking walks with his mother in the fall. Then the teacher asks students to think about and share what sounds remind them of places or things in their lives. He then breaks the class up into small groups, and he and his assistant both lead a group of students in a discussion of what sounds they hear in the classroom. The teacher follows this discussion with a walk outside to discuss the sounds the students hear outside of the classroom. One group may go to a playground where there are a lot of students, and the other group may go on a short walk along the road. When the students come back to the classroom, they have a discussion about the different things the two groups heard and how hearing can give them information about where they are. Or, during a lesson on measurement, the teacher may include a discussion of what units of measurement students would use to measure different things they encounter in their day-to-day lives: "So we have centimeters, meters, and kilometers. Which one would you use to measure the distance between your eye and your nose? Which one would you use to measure the distance between your house and school? How about the distance between the door of our room and your desk?" By relating information to students' lives, the teacher makes information much more meaningful and enhances students' ability to integrate new concepts into their everyday lives. The teacher also makes intentional efforts to use concepts and ideas that are a part of students' everyday experiences. When these opportunities are not readily available, the teacher spends time helping students connect to more abstract ideas. For example, when a reading passage uses the metaphor "she felt like she was walking on a tightrope," the teacher recognizes that most students in his classroom have never been to a circus or seen a tightrope and might not know what it is, thereby limiting their understanding of the metaphor and their comprehension of the passage. Therefore, he takes time to talk with the students about what a tightrope is and where they might see one. The teacher also has a few students who have seen a tightrope demonstrate what it might look like and feel like to walk on a tightrope.

Quality of Feedback[9]

Assesses the degree to which the teacher provides feedback that expands learning and understanding and encourages continued participation

	Low (1,2)	Mid (3,4,5)	High (6,7)
Scaffolding • Hints • Assistance	The teacher rarely provides scaffolding to students but rather dismisses responses or actions as incorrect or ignores problems in understanding.	The teacher occasionally provides scaffolding to students but at other times simply dismisses responses as incorrect or ignores problems in students' understanding.	The teacher often scaffolds for students who are having a hard time understanding a concept, answering a question, or completing an activity.
Feedback loops • Back-and-forth exchanges • Persistence by teacher • Follow-up questions	The teacher gives only perfunctory feedback to students.	There are occasional feedback loops—back-and-forth exchanges—between the teacher and students; other times, however, feedback is more perfunctory.	There are frequent feedback loops—back-and-forth exchanges—between the teacher and students.
Prompting thought processes • Asks students to explain thinking • Queries responses and actions	The teacher rarely queries the students or prompts students to explain their thinking and rationale for responses and actions.	The teacher occasionally queries the students or prompts students to explain their thinking and rationale for responses and actions.	The teacher often queries the students or prompts students to explain their thinking and rationale for responses and actions.
Providing information • Expansion • Clarification • Specific feedback	The teacher rarely provides additional information to expand on the students' understanding or actions.	The teacher occasionally provides additional information to expand on the students' understanding or actions.	The teacher often provides additional information to expand on students' understanding or actions.
Encouragement and affirmation • Recognition • Reinforcement • Student persistence	The teacher rarely offers encouragement of students' efforts that increases students' involvement and persistence.	The teacher occasionally offers encouragement of students' efforts that increases students' involvement and persistence.	The teacher often offers encouragement of students' efforts that increases students' involvement and persistence.

---

[9]Quality of Feedback is generally observed in response to a student's or students' answer to a question or as a student progresses on his or her work or involvement in an activity, whereas Concept Development is the method a teacher uses as he or she provides instruction or activities.

QUALITY OF FEEDBACK

Low Quality of Feedback (1, 2)

The teacher rarely provides scaffolding to students but rather dismisses responses or actions as incorrect or ignores problems in understanding. In scaffolding, a teacher acknowledges where a student is starting and provides the necessary level of help to allow the student to succeed or complete a task. The teacher in the low range of this dimension tends to move quickly during lessons and fails to use hints or assistance when students do not understand something or give an incorrect answer. For example, the teacher may ask a question to a large group of students; when most of the students respond out loud with the incorrect answer, she simply provides the correct answer and moves on. As another example, when asked whether a character in a story is a mom or a teacher, a student incorrectly responds "a mom." Rather than asking the student how he might know whether the character is a mom or a teacher or giving hints, the teacher simply says, "No, it's a teacher." Alternately, the teacher may completely ignore this response from the student and ask another student for her response.

The teacher gives only perfunctory feedback to students. The teacher may not interact with students in a way that allows him or her to provide feedback. For example, the teacher may spend an entire observation period reading a book and not asking questions, thus providing no opportunities for feedback. Alternately, he or she may give a great deal of feedback but focus entirely on whether an answer is correct, saying "yes," "no," or "that's not right" and moving on. Teachers at the low end of the Quality of Feedback dimension also may appear to answer all of their own questions, thus not allowing the provision of feedback on students' thoughts and ideas (e.g., "What is our main character doing in this chapter? She is looking for clues!") The teacher does not engage in a back-and-forth exchange with students intended to help them understand a specific problem or general concept or to elicit a higher level of performance.

The teacher rarely queries the students or prompts students to explain their thinking and rationale for responses and actions. When a student provides an incorrect answer, the teacher simply continues with the lesson rather than taking the time to help the student think about how she arrived at her answer or explain her thinking to other students. The teacher fails to focus on getting students to articulate their thought processes by saying things such as, "I wonder how you knew to make five groups of four instead of four groups of five" or "How did you figure out where to put that decimal point?"

The teacher rarely provides additional information to expand on the students' understanding or actions. Once a student responds to a question or completes an action, the teacher does not follow up with expansions or clarifications. For example, the teacher may ask the students to name types of fruit; after a student responds with "raisin," the teacher fails to make a comment such as, "You're right; a raisin is a fruit. It is a dried grape," but rather simply moves on. The teacher rarely provides more specific feedback about students' responses or work that might add additional knowledge and understanding for the student.

The teacher rarely offers encouragement of students' efforts that increases students' involvement and persistence. The teacher also appears to measure students' progress by how well they conform to his or her expectations by providing general praise (e.g., "nice work," "good," "great job") to the group or to individual students rather than providing students with feedback about their work process, such as how long they have been working on a project (e.g., "You have really been focused on this problem the whole math work time; how is it coming along?") or their continued efforts (e.g., "I can tell you are trying really hard to figure out your writer's plan; that is going to really help when you start writing your story"). When students are frustrated by more difficult tasks, the teacher fails to provide the encouragement that students need to persist.

Note: Classrooms receive a 1 if no feedback is given.

Middle-Range Quality of Feedback (3, 4, 5)

The teacher occasionally provides scaffolding to students but at other times simply dismisses responses as incorrect or ignores problems in students' understanding. In scaffolding, a teacher acknowledges where a student is starting and provides the necessary level of help to allow the student to succeed or complete a task. The teacher sometimes uses students' incorrect or nonresponses as an opportunity to scaffold learning by providing hints or assistance; other times she does not. For example, the teacher may be reading a book about seasons and ask many questions about what things happen in each season. During the discussion of spring, a student says that the leaves fall off the trees in the spring. The teacher says, "Remember how we talked about how it is spring right now? Are the leaves turning colors and falling off the trees? What do the trees look like right now?" As the story goes on, however, the teacher appears to tire of this more intensive feedback and simply tells the students they are incorrect or gives them the answers. As another example, as a student is working on reading a difficult word, the teacher may provide a bit of assistance, such as asking the student how he thinks the word starts; when he continues to struggle, however, she gives him the word instead of continuing to provide incremental hints or giving him more strategies to use to figure the word out himself.

There are occasional feedback loops—back-and-forth exchanges—between the teacher and students; other times, however, feedback is more perfunctory. At times, the teacher's feedback may help students to expand and elaborate on their learning, but generally these efforts by the teacher are not sustained for long. More often, the teacher simply suggests that the students' answers are feasible (e.g., "That was a good guess. Does anyone else have an idea?") and then moves on to another student. On some occasions, but not consistently, the teacher may respond to an initial student comment by engaging with the student or group of students in a sustained discussion to reach deeper understanding of concepts.

The teacher occasionally queries the students or prompts students to explain their thinking and rationale for responses and actions. In response to student comments or actions, the teacher occasionally will ask *why* questions to prompt the student to explain his or her thinking and describe his or her actions; however, this does not occur often or is typically a very brief exchange. Or, the teacher may ask the types of questions that allow students to explain what they are doing and why but then moves on before students have had ample time to respond. For example, when a student working on estimating the weight of markers and tape comments when picking up a new object, "I need to hold the tape again and see how heavy it feels!," the teacher may respond by saying, "Oh, how will feeling the tape again help you with estimating the marker's weight?" but then walk away as the student is explaining or merely nod at the student's response.

The teacher occasionally provides additional information to expand on the students' understanding or actions. The teacher sometimes goes beyond perfunctory feedback such as saying that a response is correct or incorrect, but this does not represent his or her typical style of response. Occasionally, the teacher may expand on comments, clarify incorrect responses, or provide specific feedback; other times, however, he or she does not. For example, during a whole-group activity in which students pick out rhyming word cards, the teacher may simply make statements such as, "You are all so smart" and "Wow, you guys are really good at this!" Later, however, when working on the same activity in a small group, the teacher may provide more specific feedback such as, "You said that *boat* and *coat* rhyme. You are right. Those two words sound the same in the middle and the end; they make the *oat* sound. The other word, *dog,* sounds different in the middle and end; it makes the *og* sound."

The teacher occasionally offers encouragement of students' efforts that increases students' involvement and persistence. The process of learning includes a focus on developing understanding, personal improvement, effort, persistence, and trying new strategies. Teachers in the middle range of the Quality of Feedback dimension use a mix of this process feedback and more perfunctory feedback. For example, occasionally the teacher may say, "Oh, listen to that. You are sounding the word out loud to help you spell it; what sounds do you hear in the word?" and then follow up with, "You are really working hard on using your best spelling today!" "Wow, that word sure has a lot of sounds in it; what is the first sound that you hear?" or "You are really using your letter–sound skills to make your words." Other times, however, the teacher's feedback fails to encourage the students' active involvement in the learning process. When the teacher provides encouragement, students may be observed to persist and work harder; but when this encouragement is absent, they may be less motivated to complete tasks.

High Quality of Feedback (6, 7)

Note: At the high end of the Quality of Feedback dimension, the teacher provides the following types of feedback to most of the students. However, it is possible to score at the high end of this dimension without a teacher having interactions with all students during a single observation period. Rather, during individual work time, there should be clear evidence that the teacher is providing this type of feedback to students as he or she moves around the classroom with the assumption that, over time, most students will be exposed to it. During small- or whole-group time the teacher should make attempts to get around to multiple students and provide feedback in such a way that the whole group is being exposed to it.

The teacher often scaffolds for students who are having a hard time understanding a concept, answering a question, or completing an activity. In scaffolding, a teacher acknowledges where a student is starting and provides the necessary level of help to allow the student to succeed or complete a task. The teacher in the high range of the Quality of Feedback dimension consistently provides hints or assistance to scaffold students' learning. For example, a student may be trying to figure out the number of boys and number of girls in the class and is unable to come up with the answer. The teacher may provide the student with resources and/or ask the student additional questions that will lead him or her to the answer, such as, "Let's count the number of sticks we have in the girl jar" or "Let's look at our number line and see what number comes after nine." Scaffolding also may occur as a teacher is helping the whole class solve a word problem during math. The teacher reads the problem aloud, and students begin calling out incorrect answers. Rather than simply telling them that they are wrong, the teacher says, "Hmmm, how did you get four?" and then, "It does sound like we are going to use subtraction here because I said 'she gave away,' but let's slow down and think carefully and figure out what our operation is here." As students think about the problem and call out their answers, she continues providing guidance by saying, "Oh, so we think it is actually addition? Okay, so what do you want to add?" Finally, after students have agreed on the relevant numbers, she prompts, "Sounds like we want to add 8 and 12. Does everyone agree? And what is that?" This type of feedback allows the students to perform at a higher level than they would be able to on their own.

There are frequent feedback loops—back-and-forth exchanges—between the teacher and students. There are multiple instances in which a teacher responds to a student's comment, action, or performance by engaging with the student in a sustained back-and-forth exchange with the intention of helping him or her really understand ideas or get to the correct answer. The teacher persists in these efforts rather than just stopping with one clarifying comment. The teacher may ask questions that help the student engage in the discussion of his or her work, which promotes further learning and thinking on the part of the student. At the high end of the Quality of Feedback dimension, the teacher often uses students' responses or spontaneous comments to create a learning moment by asking follow-up questions to facilitate a higher level of understanding or performance from the students. These feedback loops can occur either in the context of discussion of big concepts and ideas or in the context of helping students get to one correct answer. For example, during a discussion about how to resolve conflicts with peers, the teacher incorporates students' ideas and suggestions while at the same time asking questions about why certain comments are helpful or unhelpful, whether students have ever felt particular ways during conflicts, what they did when they felt that way, what helped them feel better, and so forth. This conversation helps students understand more about the answers they provide. A teacher also may be involved in a discussion that has a correct answer. For example, she may be working with a student individually on reading and ask the student, "What do you think this word is?" When the student does not respond, the teacher follows up with, "What letter do you see at the beginning of the word? Is it just one letter or a blend?" The student says "B." The teacher responds by saying, "Is it just the *B,* or is it one of our blends? Let's look at our word wall. What is our blend this week?" The student looks at the blend posted on the word wall and the word in the book and says, "*Br,* this has the *br.*" The teacher says, "Nice work. What sound does our *br* blend make?" and proceeds to help the student figure out what the word is.

The teacher often queries the students or prompts students to explain their thinking and rationale for responses and actions. In response to students' comments or actions, the teacher often asks *why* questions that prompt the students to explain their thinking. For example, after asking a student to pass out alphabet cards to her peers, a teacher notices that the student is passing them out to students whose name starts with that letter (e.g., *A* to Alvin, *B* to Briana). The teacher capitalizes on this learning moment by asking the student why she is passing out cards in this way. Or, during a science experiment on light, the teacher observes a group of students holding an object under the table (where it is darker) to shine the flashlight on it and asks them to explain why they are doing this and how it helps them understand how light interacts with the object. This type of feedback, in which teachers ask questions about why students are doing something or how they arrived at a particular answer, helps all students in the classroom understand the process of learning. For example, the teacher may ask students to look at their wall weather chart and tell her whether they have had more cloudy or sunny days. A student responds with "cloudy." Rather than simply saying, "You're right," the teacher follows up by asking, "How did you know it was cloudy?" The student then explains that he used the chart on the wall and looked at which line was longer; the teacher follows up by saying that the lines show how many cloudy and sunny days there have been and that the longer lines indicate more cloudy days.

The teacher often provides additional information to expand on students' understanding or actions. The teacher consistently goes beyond simply saying that a response is correct or incorrect. The teacher may expand on an initial student behavior or response. For example, the teacher may be working with a small group of students to plant seeds in pots. One student pours too much water into the pot, and the teacher says, "Wow, you put a lot of water in there. When you put that much water in the pot the dirt gets so wet that the seed can't grow very well. Let's try it again with a little less water so that the seed can grow up to be a plant." Or, during a small-group lesson in which students are sorting foods, a student puts a banana in the fruit bin. The teacher then says, "Ah, I see you put the banana in the fruit bin. You're right, the banana is a fruit just like an orange and a pear because they are sweet and fleshy." The teacher also may provide clarification after a student gives a partially correct or incorrect response: "I heard you make the /th/ sound at the beginning of that word—way to go!—but let's look at the end sound more closely." At the high end of this dimension, the teacher frequently gives this type of very specific feedback that is individualized to specific students or contexts of learning rather than providing global "good job" types of feedback.

The teacher often offers encouragement of students' efforts that increases students' involvement and persistence. The teacher's primary concern when giving feedback is to increase students' understanding, personal improvement, effort and persistence or get students to try new strategies. When students are presenting their work to the whole group, the teacher may respond when they are finished by saying, "That was really great! I really like how you all stood up and held your poster so that the whole class could see it and spoke loudly and clearly so that everyone could hear what you were saying. That was a great way to present your work!" The teacher focuses attention on effort and explicitly recognizes students' efforts by saying things such as, "Wow, you are really trying hard to figure this out," "Tell me about your story—how did you decide what your opening sentence was going to be?" or "Wow, you made a lot of different colors on your picture with the tissue paper; how did you do that?" If a student appears to be getting frustrated, the teacher offers reinforcement and encouragement by making statements such as, "This is a hard one, but let's keep going; you are on the right track, and I think you can do it." As a result of these interactions, students in this classroom are able to persist even when working on more difficult tasks.

Language Modeling[10]

Captures the quality and amount of the teacher's use of language-stimulation and language-facilitation techniques

	Low (1,2)	Mid (3,4,5)	High (6,7)
Frequent conversation • Back-and-forth exchanges • Contingent responding • Peer conversations	There are few if any conversations in the classroom.	There are limited conversations in the classroom.	There are frequent conversations in the classroom.
Open-ended questions • Questions require more than a one-word response • Students respond	The majority of the teacher's questions are closed-ended.	The teacher asks a mix of closed-ended and open-ended questions.	The teacher asks many open-ended questions.
Repetition and extension • Repeats • Extends/elaborates	The teacher rarely, if ever, repeats or extends the students' responses.	The teacher sometimes repeats or extends the students' responses.	The teacher often repeats or extends the students' responses.
Self- and parallel talk • Maps own actions with language • Maps student action with language	The teacher rarely maps his or her own actions and the students' actions through language and description.	The teacher occasionally maps his or her own actions and the students' actions through language and description.	The teacher consistently maps his or her own actions and the students' actions through language and description.
Advanced language • Variety of words • Connected to familiar words and/or ideas	The teacher does not use advanced language with students.	The teacher sometimes uses advanced language with students.	The teacher often uses advanced language with students.

[10]In classrooms that may be considered bilingual, the teacher may move between speaking in English and Spanish. However, speaking two languages in the classroom does not increase the rating of Language Modeling independent of using indicators under "High." Therefore, it is expected that teachers in bilingual classrooms that are rated "High" will be engaging in frequent conversation, asking open-ended questions, and so forth, regardless of the language used. A teacher who repeats book as both "book" and "libro" or water as "water" and "agua" to children should not be rated higher than a teacher who uses only the word "book" or "water."

LANGUAGE MODELING

Low Language Modeling (1, 2)

There are few if any conversations in the classroom. Few individual, small-group, and/or large-group conversations occur between the students and the teacher. In classrooms at the low end of the Language Modeling dimension, the teacher rarely initiates conversations with students and does not engage conversationally with students, either during instruction as part of lessons or during "down time" moments. If students talk to the teacher, the teacher rarely responds with more than a few words. In addition, there are few, if any, back-and-forth exchanges between the teacher and students. The conversations that do occur in the classroom are primarily teacher-controlled and focus on students' behavior, classroom management, or teaching a particular concept or skill. Teacher-controlled conversations are those in which the teacher selects the conversational topic, limits students' answers, and/or does not wait patiently for students to respond. For instance, a group instruction time for a classroom scoring at the low end of this dimension would include a preponderance of closed-ended questions and little recasting or repeating of students' responses, such as the following:

Teacher: How many groups do we have in this problem?

[Students chorally respond.]

Teacher: Good. Now how many items in each group?

[Students chorally respond.]

Teacher: Good job. So what does that give us?

[Students chorally respond.]

Teacher: That's right. Nice work.

In this interaction, the students have little or no opportunity to initiate conversation; the teacher is setting the pace and the conversational focus, no extended turn taking is present, and the students' communicative participation is highly constrained. Classrooms receiving a low score on this dimension are characterized by a high frequency of this type of teacher–student interaction. Students do not initiate conversation with their peers, and rarely, if ever, engage in extended conversations with one another. The students primarily direct their comments to the teacher.

The majority of the teacher's questions are closed-ended. The teacher consistently asks questions that require no more than a one-word answer or short sentence (e.g., "What shape is this?" "What is our word of the week?" "How many are there?") Students rarely, if ever, have opportunities to respond to the teacher with more complex language.

The teacher rarely, if ever, repeats or extends the students' responses. When students make comments or ask questions, the teacher does not respond to the comment or answer the question and/or ignores the student's communicative attempt. For example, while the teacher is reading a book to the class, a student points to and makes a com-

LANGUAGE
MODELING

ment about the illustration: "She is looking for the dog, and he is right around the corner where she can't see." The teacher either continues to read, ignoring the student's comment, or simply says "Yes."

The teacher rarely maps his or her own actions and the students' actions through language and description. The teacher does not use self-talk or parallel talk in conversation or instruction. For example, when he is writing something up on the board, he simply writes, rather than using it as an opportunity to link his actions to language by saying something such as, "Now I am writing a *B,* then an *O,* then an *A,* then a *T.*" Or, "Okay, that was a suggestion for how we would end our story, so I am going to write it down here by *Conclusion.*" During interactions with students, he fails to use parallel talk to describe what the students are doing, such as, "Wow you are being really organized with your materials for your car; you are putting your wheel parts over here and the body parts over here" or "You are looking so carefully to see if the scale is balanced. You are even bending down so that you can get a better angle."

The teacher does not use advanced language with students. The vocabulary that the teacher uses to explain concepts to the students is limited and lacks variety. Terms or ideas that may be difficult for students are rarely clarified in simpler terms or in a way to which students can relate.

Middle-Range Language Modeling (3, 4, 5)

There are limited conversations in the classroom. The teacher talks regularly with and to the students and appears somewhat interested in the students; however, conversations typically are limited to one or two back-and-forth exchanges rather than developing into prolonged conversations. For example, consider the following exchange during which the teacher and student are taking a picture walk through a book together:

Teacher: Tell me what is on this page.

Student: A man is walking.

Teacher: Where do you think he is walking?

Student: I don't know.

Teacher: Hmm. Okay. [Turns page]

Although students will on occasion initiate conversation or make comments that invite discussion, teacher-initiated interactions tend to predominate. Discussions may focus on topics or areas of interest to the students, but the teacher often is directing the conversation. At times, this is necessary so that students do not wander off topic. However, teachers in the middle range of the Language Modeling dimension do not always acknowledge or follow a student's conversational lead even when the student is initiating conversation that is relevant to the topic at hand. For example, when discussing homophones with different spellings (e.g., *to, too,* and *two*), a student asks what it is called when one word has two different meanings with the same spelling (such as *bark*). Instead of responding to the student's question and clarifying the difference between homographs and homophones for the whole class, the teacher simply says, "We aren't talking about that today; we are talking about homophones." Students also occasionally may engage in conversations with one another. More often, basic information is exchanged between students such as simple requests, comments, or protests (e.g., "Can I use the glue when you are done?" "You go first"). Once initiated, there may be a few conversational turns but not extended conversation.

The teacher asks a mix of closed-ended and open-ended questions. The teacher sometimes asks questions that require the students to use more complex language; however, the majority of questions are closed-ended and require only short responses from the students. For example, the teacher might have the following discussion with students about the weather patterns on the board:

Teacher: What is this?

Students: Sun.

Teacher: What is this?

Students: Rain.

Teacher: How can we tell what the weather might be like today?

In this interaction, the teacher has asked a series of "test" questions followed by an open-ended question requiring the students to respond with more than a single word. Interactions such as this occur occasionally in the middle range of this dimension, but often the students' responses are limited by the types of questions the teacher asks.

The teacher sometimes repeats or extends the students' responses. When students make comments, the teacher sometimes acknowledges these responses by repeating them or offering a bit more information or language; other times, however, the teacher ignores these comments. Often, there is a mix of responding and ignoring.

The teacher occasionally maps his or her own actions and the students' actions through language and description. The teacher sometimes uses self-talk and parallel talk to model language for students; however, in the middle range of this dimension, the teacher uses these strategies only occasionally. For example, as he is getting ready for a lesson, the teacher may use self-talk, saying, "I'm getting out my notebook and getting all of the books ready for us to use." He may use parallel talk to describe what the students are doing: "Lena, I see you are working hard on your Gallon Man. You are making the body first, labeling it *G* for gallon, then the arms and legs, labeling those with *Qt.* for quart." Again, in the middle range of this dimension, these strategies are not used consistently.

The teacher sometimes uses advanced language with students. The teacher may use a variety of nouns, adjectives, verbs, and vocabulary terms to explain or clarify information. Sometimes he or she may map these onto known concepts (e.g., "Hexagon, the stop sign shape") and other times he or she may not.

High Language Modeling (6, 7)

Note: At the high end of the Language Modeling dimension, the teacher provides the types of learning opportunities discussed in this section to most of the students. It is possible, however, for a teacher to score at the high end of this dimension without interacting with all of students during a single observation period. Rather, during individual work time, there should be clear evidence that the teacher is engaging in these types of language interactions with students as he moves around the classroom with the assumption that, over time, most students will be exposed to them. During small- or whole-group time, the teacher should make attempts to get around to multiple students and provide language-stimulating techniques in such a way that the whole group is exposed to them.

There are frequent conversations in the classroom. Many conversations occur between students and the teacher and among students that promote opportunities for language use. In classrooms at the high end of this dimension, the teacher often initiates conversations with students; in addition, there is a natural flow in the exchange of information during center time or other open periods of time that encourages students to converse and makes them feel as if they are valued conversational partners. The conversation is engaging for students because the teacher actively listens, contributes relevant responses, and asks related questions. In addition, the teacher provides a format that allows students to initiate questions and commentaries and respond in extended sentences to questions. The teacher in this classroom also sets the tone for periods of time during which students should not be communicating and the teacher is in charge. For instance, the teacher may read a book and explain to students that their job is to listen carefully while he is reading; they can talk about the book later. Or, the teacher may temporarily ask students not to raise their hands and hold their comments until he is finished talking. To receive a high score on this scale, however, these teacher-controlled periods should be relatively short, and the teacher should then make a transition to a period in which he or she encourages more student talk. In classrooms on the high end of the Language Modeling dimension, students also engage in extended conversations with one another. Students initiate conversations with their peers and seek one another to talk. There is joint discussion regarding materials, procedures, and concepts during group work activities. Requests for necessary materials are made with little teacher involvement or independently. Students make comments describing each other's work or behaviors and engage in discussion with peers about what they are learning together.

The teacher asks many open-ended questions. Open-ended questions are those that invite elaborate responses such as, "Tell me about…" or "Share your story with the group." Often, these are questions for which the answer is unknown, such as, "What do you think?" or "How do you know?" Questions also may have a known answer (e.g., "Tell me what is happening on this page?"); however, the important consideration for this dimension is that the teacher asks open-ended questions that require students to put together language to communicate more complex ideas. Consider the following exchange between a teacher and student discussing the student's writing project:

Student: I think I am finished with my book.

Teacher: Wow, tell me about it.

Student: It's called "The Great Adventure of Sparky and Ben." Ben is the main character and Sparky is his sidekick, his dog. They are best friends.

Teacher: Neat. The title makes me think it's going to be an action book. Is that accurate? What is your plot?

The teacher often repeats or extends the students' responses. In high-quality language environments, the teacher focuses first on students' attempts to communicate and then builds directly on the student's contribution. The following is an example of *extending:*

[The teacher shows the student a picture of zebras in a book.]

Teacher: What do you see here?

Student: A big group of zebras!

Teacher: Yes, it's a big group of zebras. It's called a herd of zebras.

Student: Like a herd of cows?

Teacher: Yes, like that. Sometimes groups of animals are called a herd. Other times, they are called other things; a group of fish is called a school, a group of dogs is called a pack, and a group of birds is called a flock.

In the following example of *repeating,* a student brings the teacher his worksheet:

Student: I finished my handwriting.

Teacher: You finished your handwriting! Alright, now that that is complete, what will you do next?

In both of these examples, the teacher acknowledges the student's comments. He also affirms the student's observations and recasts the information in a more complex form. At the high end of this dimension, the teacher may not follow up on every single student comment, but the majority of student comments are responded to in some way.

The teacher consistently maps his or her own actions and the students' actions through language and description. Many times during whole-group instruction, center time, and even periods such as snack and transitions in and out of the room, the teacher uses self-talk and parallel talk as a means of expanding the students' language. In self-talk, the teacher simply says what he or she is doing, linking words to actions: "I'm checking to see that you are all ready to listen, and I see that you are. So, I can get out my book and start reading. I'm looking for our bookmark—where we left off yesterday. Okay, now I'll start reading Chapter 7." In parallel talk, the teacher provides language for students' actions: "You are picking up the rubber bands and putting them back away so carefully. You are getting them all back in the box so that they will be ready to go next time we use the geoboards."

The teacher often uses advanced language with the students. Teachers in classrooms that score on the high end of the Language Modeling dimension use a variety of nouns, verbs, adverbs, adjectives, prepositions, and other forms of language that are new to the students but that map onto concepts already understood by the students. There is an explicit attempt to extend students' understanding of these parts of language. Consider the following example in which the teacher maps the student's language about geometric shapes into a slightly more sophisticated form and summarizes the student's response by using new or unfamiliar vocabulary:

Teacher: What shapes do you see in this picture?

Student: A diamond shape.

Teacher: Yes, a diamond shape. It is also called a rhombus. That's a big second-grade word for that shape.

In the following example, the teacher clarifies a new or unfamiliar vocabulary term as it relates to an everyday object with which the students are familiar:

Teacher: [reading from a book] "It's time to seal your shell and sleep." What is she going to do if she seals her shell?

Student: Get inside her shell.

Teacher: That's right. Just like how we seal a Ziploc bag. You know how to do that. She is going to seal her shell nice and tight so that nothing can get in and nothing can get out. She will stay nice and warm.

References

Anderson, L., Evertson, C., & Emmer, E. (1980). Dimensions in classroom management derived from recent research. *Journal of Curriculum Studies, 12,* 343–356.

Blair, C. (2002). School readiness: Integrating cognition and emotion in a neurobiological conceptualization of children's functioning at school entry. *American Psychologist, 57*(2), 111–127.

Blair, C. (2003). Behavioral inhibition and behavioral activation in young children: Relations with self-regulation and adaptation to preschool in children attending Head Start. *Developmental Psychobiology, 42*(3), 301–311.

Bogard, K., & Takanishi, R. (2005). PK–3: An aligned and coordinated approach to education for children 3 to 8 years old. *Social Policy Report: A Publication of the Society for Research in Child Development, 19*(3), 1–24.

Bowman, B., & Stott, F. (1994). Understanding development in a cultural context: The challenge for teachers. In B. Mallory & R. New (Eds.), *Diversity and developmentally appropriate practices: Challenges for early childhood education* (pp. 19–34). New York: Teachers College Press.

Brophy, J., & Evertson, C. (1976). *Learning from teaching: A developmental perspective.* Boston: Allyn and Bacon.

Brophy, J.E., & Good, T.L. (1986). Teacher behavior and student achievement. In M.C. Wittrock (Ed.), *Handbook of research on teaching* (3rd edition, pp. 328–375). New York: Macmillan.

Bruner, J. (1996). *The culture of education.* Cambridge, MA: Harvard University Press.

Bryant, D., Clifford, R., Early, D., Pianta, R., Howes, C., Barbarin, O., et al. (2002, November). *Findings from the NCEDL Multi-State Pre-Kindergarten Study.* Paper presented at the annual meeting of the National Association for the Education of Young Children, New York.

Catts, H.W., Fey, M.E., Zhang, X., & Tomblin, J.B. (1999). Language basis of reading and reading disabilities: Evidence from a longitudinal investigation. *Scientific Studies of Reading, 3*(4), 331–361.

Coker, H., Medley, D.M., & Soar, R.S. (1980). How valid are expert opinions about effective teaching? *Phi Delta Kappan, 62*(2), 131–134, 149.

Davis, E.A., & Miyake, N. (2004). Explorations of scaffolding in complex classroom systems. *Journal of the Learning Sciences, 13*(3), 265–272.

Denham, S.A., & Weissberg, R.P. (2004). Social-emotional learning in early childhood: What we know and where to go from here. In E. Chesebrough, P. King, T.P. Gullotta, & M. Bloom (Eds.), *A blueprint for the promotion of prosocial behavior in early childhood* (pp. 13–50). New York: Kluwer Academic/Plenum.

Early, D., Barbarin, O., Bryant, D., Burchinal, M., Chang, F., Clifford, R., et al. (2005). *Prekindergarten in eleven states: NCEDL's Multi-State Study of Pre-Kindergarten and Study of State-Wide Early Education Programs.* Retrieved December 1, 2005, from http://www.fpg.unc.edu/NCEDL/pdfs/SWEEP_MS_summary_final.pdf

Emmer, E.T., & Stough, L. (2001). Classroom management: A critical part of educational psychology, with implications for teacher education. *Educational Psychologist, 36*(2), 103–112.

Evertson, C., Emmer, E., Sanford, J., & Clements, B. (1983). Improving classroom management: An experiment in elementary classrooms. *Elementary School Journal, 84,* 173–188.

Evertson, C., & Harris, A. (1999). Support for managing learning-centered classrooms: The classroom organization and management program. In H.J. Freiberg (Ed.), *Beyond behaviorism: Changing the classroom management paradigm* (pp. 59–74). Boston: Allyn & Bacon.

Fujiki, M., Brinton, B., & Clarke, D. (2002). Emotion regulation in children with specific language impairment. *Language, Speech, and Hearing Services in Schools, 33*, 102–111.

Good, T., & Grouws, D. (1977). Teaching effects: A process-product study of fourth grade mathematics classrooms. *Journal of Teacher Education, 28*, 49–54.

Greenberg, M.T., Domitrovich, C., & Bumbarger, B. (2001). The prevention of mental disorders in school-aged children: Current state of the field. *Prevention and Treatment, 4.*

Greenberg, M.T., Weissberg, R.P., & O'Brien, M.U. (2003). Enhancing school-based prevention and youth development through coordinated social, emotional, and academic learning. *American Psychologist, 58*(6–7), 466–474.

Hamre, B.K., Mashburn, A., Pianta, R.C., & Downer, J. (2006). *Validation of 3-factor model for classroom quality across preschool to fifth grade.* Manuscript submitted for publication.

Hamre, B.K., & Pianta, R.C. (2001). Early teacher–child relationships and the trajectory of children's school outcomes through eighth grade. *Child Development, 72*(2), 625–638.

Hamre, B.K., & Pianta, R.C. (2005). Can instructional and emotional support in the first grade classroom make a difference for children at risk of school failure? *Child Development, 76*(5), 949–967.

Hamre, B.K., & Pianta, R.C. (2007). Learning opportunities in preschool and early elementary classrooms. In R.C. Pianta, M.J. Cox, & K.L. Snow (Eds.), *School readiness and the transition to kindergarten in the era of accountability* (pp. 49–83). Baltimore: Paul H. Brookes Publishing Co.

Howes, C., Burchinal, M., Pianta, R.C., Bryant, D., Early, D., Clifford, R., et al. (in press). Ready to learn? Children's pre-academic achievement in pre-kindergarten programs. *Early Childhood Research Quarterly.*

Illinois State Board of Education. (2004). *Illinois learning standards—social/emotional learning (SEL).* Retrieved February 16, 2006, from http://www.isbe.net/ils/social_emotional/standards.htm

Kounin, J.S. (1970). *Discipline and group management in classrooms.* Austin, TX: Holt, Rhinehart & Winston.

Ladd, G.W., Birch, S.H., & Buhs, E.S. (1999). Children's social and scholastic lives in kindergarten: Related spheres of influence? *Child Development, 70*, 1373–1400.

La Paro, K.M, & Pianta, R.C. (2000). Predicting children's competence in the early school years: A meta-analytic review. *Review of Educational Research, 70*(4), 443–484.

La Paro, K.M., Pianta, R.C., & Stuhlman, M. (2004, May). The Classroom Assessment Scoring System: Findings from the prekindergarten year. *The Elementary School Journal, 104*(5), 409–426.

Mashburn, A.J., Hamre, B.K., Downer, J.T., Pianta, R.C. (2007). Teacher and classroom characteristics associated with teachers' ratings of pre-kindergartners' relationships and behaviors. *Journal of Psychoeducational Assessment, 24*(4), 367–380.

Mashburn, A.J., Pianta, R.C., Hamre, B.K., Downer, J.T., Barbarin, O., Bryant, D., Burchinal, M., et al. (in press). Pre-k program standards and children's development of academic and language skills. *Child Development.*

Morrison, F.J., & Connor, C.M. (2002). Understanding schooling effects on early literacy: A working research strategy. *Journal of School Psychology, 40*(6), 493–500.

National Research Council. (1999). *How people learn: Brain, mind, experience, and school.* Washington, DC: National Academies Press.

NICHD Early Child Care Research Network. (2002). The relation of global first grade classroom environment to structural classroom features, teacher, and student behaviors. *Elementary School Journal, 102*(5), 367–387.

NICHD Early Child Care Research Network. (2003). Social functioning in first grade: Prediction from home, child care and concurrent school experience. *Child Development, 74*, 1639–1662.

NICHD Early Child Care Research Network. (2005). A day in third grade: A large-scale study of classroom quality and teacher and student behavior. *The Elementary School Journal, 105*, 305–323.

Pianta, R.C. (2003, February). *Teacher–child interactions: The implications of observational research for re-designing professional development.* Presentation to the Science and Ecology of Early Development (SEED), National Institute of Child Health and Human Development, Washington, DC.

Pianta, R.C. (2006). Teacher–child relationships and early literacy. In D. Dickinson & S. Newman (Eds.), *Handbook of early literacy research* (Vol. 2, pp. 149–162). New York: The Guilford Press.

Pianta, R.C., La Paro, K.M., & Hamre, B.K. (2004). *Classroom Assessment Scoring System (CLASS).* Unpublished measure, University of Virginia.

Pianta, R.C., La Paro, K.M., Payne, C., Cox, M.J., & Bradley, R. (2002). The relation of kindergarten classroom environment to teacher, family, and school characteristics and child outcomes. *Elementary School Journal, 102*(3), 225–238.

Pianta, R.C., Steinberg, M.S., & Rollins, K.B. (1995). The first two years of school: Teacher–child relationships and deflections in children's classroom adjustment. *Development and Psychopathology, 7,* 295–312.

Pintrich, P.R. (2000). The role of goal orientation in self-regulated learning. In M. Boekaerts, P.R. Pintrich, and M. Zeidner (Eds.), *Handbook of self-regulation* (pp. 451–502). San Diego: Academic Press.

Raver, C.C. (2004). Placing emotional self-regulation in sociocultural and socioeconomic contexts. *Child Development, 75*(2), 346–353.

Rogoff, B. (1990). *Apprenticeship in thinking: Cognitive development in social context.* New York, NY: Oxford University Press.

Romberg, T.A., Carpenter, T.P., & Dremock, F. (2005). *Understanding mathematics and science matters.* Mahwah, NJ: Lawrence Erlbaum Associates.

Rutter, M., & Maughan, B. (2002). School effectiveness findings, 1979–2002. *Journal of School Psychology, 40*(6), 451–475.

Sanford, J., & Evertson, C. (1981). Classroom management in a low SES junior high: Three case studies. *Journal of Teacher Education, 32*(1), 34–38.

Schunk, D.H. (2005). Self-regulated learning: The educational legacy of Paul R. Pintrich. *Educational Psychologist, 40*(2), 85–94.

Silver, R.B., Measelle, J., Essex, M., & Armstrong, J.M. (2005). Trajectories of externalizing behavior problems in the classroom: Contributions of child characteristics, family characteristics, and the teacher–child relationship during the school transition. *Journal of School Psychology, 43,* 39–60.

Skibbe, L., Behnke, M., & Justice, L.M. (2004). Parental scaffolding of children's phonological awareness skills: Interactions between mothers and their preschoolers with language difficulties. *Communication Disorders Quarterly, 25*(4), 189–203.

Soar, R., & Soar, R. (1979). Emotional climate and management. In P. Peterson & H. Walberg (Eds.), *Research on teaching: Concepts, findings, and implications* (pp. 97–119). Berkeley, CA: McCutchan.

Sperling, R.A., Howard, B.C., & Staley, R. (2004). Metacognition and self-regulated learning constructs. *Educational Research and Evaluation, 10*(2), 117–139.

Stallings, J. (1975). Implementation and child effects of teaching practices in follow through classrooms. *Monographs of the Society for Research in Child Development, 40*(7–8, Serial No. 163).

Stallings, J., Cory, R., Fairweather, J., & Needels, M. (1978). *Early childhood education classroom evaluation.* Menlo Park, CA: SRI International.

Taylor, B.M., Pearson, P.D., Peterson, D.S., & Rodriguez, M.C. (2003). Reading growth in high-poverty classrooms: The influence of teacher practices that encourage cognitive engagement in literacy learning. *The Elementary School Journal, 104,* 3–28.

Veenman, M.V.J., Kok, R., & Blöte, A.W. (2005). The relation between intellectual and metacognitive skills in early adolescence. *Instructional Science, 33*(3), 193–211.

Vygotsky, L.S. (1978). *Mind and society: The development of higher mental processes.* Cambridge, MA: Harvard University Press.

Vygotsky, L.S. (1991). Genesis of the higher mental functions. In P. Light, S. Sheldon, & M. Woodhead (Eds.), *Learning to think* (pp. 32–41). Florence, KY: Taylor & Frances/Routledge.

Wharton-McDonald, R., Pressley, M., & Hampston, J.M. (1998). Literacy instruction in nine first-grade classrooms: Teacher characteristics and student achievement. *Elementary School Journal, 99*(2), 101–128.

Williams, W.M., Blythe, T., & White, N. (2002). Practical intelligence for school: Developing metacognitive sources of achievement in adolescence. *Developmental Review, 22*(2), 162–210.

Yair, G. (2000). Educational battlefields in America: The tug-of-war over students' engagement with instruction. *Sociology of Education, 73,* 247–269.

Zins, J.E., Bloodworth, M.R., Weissberg, R.P., & Walberg, H. (2004). The scientific base linking social and emotional learning to school success. In J.E. Zins, R.P. Weissberg, M.C. Wang, & H.J. Walberg, (Eds.), *Building academic success on social and emotional learning: What does the research say?* New York: Teachers College Press.

Technical Appendix

The Classroom Assessment Scoring System® (CLASS®) is an observational instrument developed to assess classroom quality in preschool through third-grade classrooms. This technical appendix provides information on the psychometric properties of the CLASS, including descriptive statistics and information about the measure's reliability and validity. Two versions of the CLASS are in broad use: a preschool version and a K–3 version. Several studies have used the K–3 version to observe classrooms up through sixth grade. In addition, there are pilot versions of the CLASS-Infant/Toddler and CLASS-Secondary. Data on the secondary pilot version are not included in this manual, but more information is available from the authors (contact Bridget Hamre, Ph.D., at hamre@virginia.edu). The data on the CLASS will be periodically updated. Please check www.classobservation.com for updates.

The intent of this technical manual is to provide information on the CLASS's technical properties based on available data and samples and to answer questions about the CLASS (e.g., How long should the observation window be for reliable assessment?). Much of this information will be drawn from studies that were done using the CLASS; however, some of the information related to these questions is based on the Classroom Observation System (COS; NICHD ECCRN, 2002), a precursor to the CLASS that was used in the first, third, and fifth grades in the National Institute of Child Health and Human Development (NICHD) Study of Early Child Care and Youth Development (SECCYD) (NICHD ECCRN, 2002). The NICHD study observations are relevant to the CLASS because 1) many of the scales used in the NICHD study are similar in nature and scaling (7-point ratings) to the CLASS and 2) the NICHD study addressed many of the technical issues that are relevant to the CLASS and addressed in this manual. The NICHD data are summarized in the following sections; more detailed information can be found in the papers that were published using these data and in materials available on the project web site (http://www.secc.rti.org).

The CLASS and COS have been used to observe more than 4,000 classrooms across the United States and, as such, represent two of the most extensively used observational measures for preschool through elementary classrooms. As described in detail in the text that follows, these are well-validated tools that provide evidence that classrooms that obtain higher scores on these two scoring systems have students who make greater academic and social progress during the school year. Both systems have standard training procedures available to ensure a high degree of reliability across coders, and ample evidence indicates that they provide reliable estimates of classroom quality, even when the classrooms are observed for just a few hours. The following sections provide a brief overview of and technical information about the CLASS.

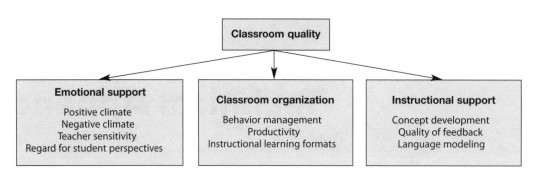

Figure A.1. Overview of CLASS domains and dimensions.

OVERVIEW OF THE CLASS

The CLASS dimensions are based on development theory and research suggesting that interactions between students and adults are the primary mechanism of student development and learning (Greenberg, Domitrovich, & Bumbarger, 2001; Hamre & Pianta, 2007; Morrison & Connor, 2002; Pianta, 2006; Rutter & Maughan, 2002). The CLASS dimensions are based on interactions between and among teachers and students in classrooms; scoring for the dimensions is not determined by the presence of materials, the physical environment or safety, or the adoption of a specific curriculum. This distinction between *observed interactions* and physical materials or reported use of curriculum is important because in most early elementary settings, materials and curriculum are usually prevalent and fairly well organized. In the CLASS, the focus is on what teachers *do* with the materials they have and on the interactions the teachers have with the students.

At the broadest level, interactions between teachers and students can be grouped into three domains: Emotional Support, Classroom Organization, and Instructional Support. Figure A.1 provides an overview of these domains and the dimensions within each domain that are measured by the CLASS. This organizational structure for classroom interactions has been validated in more than 3,000 classrooms from preschool to fifth grade (Hamre, Mashburn, Pianta, & Downer, 2006).

In the CLASS approach, the domains and dimensions used to define classroom quality and on which classrooms are assessed are common across the preschool to third-grade period. However, the ways these dimensions are manifested and demonstrated are specific to particular developmental levels or age groups (i.e., preschool versus grades K–3). In this way, the CLASS approach provides a common metric and language for the discussion of quality across grades, thereby addressing problems with grade-to-grade transition and the need for coherence (Bogard & Takanishi, 2005). However, the dimensions still provide a context-specific and developmentally sensitive metric for each grade level.

STUDIES PROVIDING CLASSROOM OBSERVATION DATA

The information included in this technical manual is drawn from multiple samples, each of which is described briefly next.

National Center for Early Development and Learning Multi-State Study of Prekindergarten and State-Wide Early Education Programs Study

Primary Investigator: NCEDL, University of North Carolina, University of Virginia, University of California—Los Angeles)

Study summary: NCEDL has conducted two major studies of state-funded preschool programs aimed at understanding variations among preschool programs and examining how these variations relate to children's academic and social development through first grade: the six-state Multi-State Study of Prekindergarten and the five-state State-Wide Early Education Programs (SWEEP) study (Early et al., 2005).

Number of classrooms: 694 preschool and 730 kindergarten

Location: Preschools in 11 states (Multi-State and SWEEP studies combined); kindergartens in 6 states (Multi-State study only)

Sampling: Random sample of preschool classrooms across states or a major geographic area within states; kindergarten classrooms attended by children in the preschool sample

Time of year: Fall and spring

Observation procedure: Unless otherwise noted, the CLASS scores reported here were averaged across data collected in the fall and spring. During the preschool year, observers were in classrooms all day for half-day programs and until naptime in full-day programs. Most classrooms were observed for 2 days. The CLASS was scored at regular intervals throughout the 2 days, with the average classroom being observed for 15 intervals. During each interval, coders took CLASS related notes and spent part of the time collecting data on other related measures. Within each interval, 5-minute blocks focused exclusively on observing for the CLASS. This same process was repeated in kindergartens.

MyTeachingPartner Study

(Primary Investigator: Dr. Robert Pianta, University of Virginia)

Study summary: MyTeachingPartner (MTP; Pianta et al., 2007) is an innovative professional development approach that uses a collaborative consultation process and web-based resources to provide ongoing, classroom-focused in-service training at a statewide level.

Number of classrooms: 164 preschool

Location: Virginia

Sampling: Teachers who agreed to participate within randomly selected districts

Time of year: Throughout one academic year (August to June) in 2-week intervals

Observation procedure: Teachers were asked to send in videotapes every 2 weeks over the course of year. These videotapes alternated between a literacy or language activity and an activity from a social-emotional development curriculum. Teachers were asked to send in at least 30 minutes of video that included an activity as well as some time before and after the activity. Trained graduate students coded these videos using the CLASS. Data reported here are from the first year of the intervention.

4Rs Program

(Primary Investigator: Dr. Lawrence Aber, New York University)

Study summary: Eighteen New York City elementary schools were identified to participate in a major study of the effects of social-emotional learning and literacy development programs on students in grades 3–5. This study was designed to help teachers and school officials learn about the best ways to promote children's reading abilities, positive behaviors, and social interactions. The specific aim of this study was to evaluate the impact of The 4Rs Program—the four *R*s being Reading, Writing, Respect, and Resolution—on students and teachers.

Number of classrooms: 82

Location: New York City

Sampling: A total of 18 schools were selected to participate in this study. Nine of the schools were randomly assigned to participate in The 4Rs Program (that is, to be the intervention schools); the other nine were assigned to a control group and agreed not to implement The 4Rs Program until data collection for the study was completed.

Time of year: Fall

Observation procedure: Observations occurred in the fall and consisted of approximately four 20-minute observation cycles, typically starting at the beginning of the school day.

Responsive Classroom Approach

(Primary Investigator: Dr. Sara Rimm Kaufman, University of Virginia)

Study summary: Data for the Social and Academic Learning Study were collected as part of a 3-year quasi-experimental study of the Responsive Classroom Approach. The Responsive Classroom Approach, developed by the Northeast Foundation for Children, is an approach to elementary school teaching that integrates academic with social learning, prioritizes caring between teachers and children and among children themselves, and offers teachers a set of principles and practices to guide classroom management, instruction, and organization.

Number of classrooms: 88

Location: An urban district in the Northeast

Sampling: Participants were in schools that used the Responsive Classroom Approach and in a matched comparison group in the same district. Participants taught grades 1–5, with between 11 and 16 teachers corresponding to each grade level. The schools, on average, had 53.63% of students who were ethnic minorities (Responsive Classroom schools had 50.56%; the comparison group had 56.70%) and 35.32% who were eligible for free or reduced-price lunches (Responsive Classroom schools had 34.46%; the comparison group had 36.17%).

Time of year: October through April

Observation procedure: A trained observer went to each classroom one time between October and April. Observations began first thing in the morning after at least three quarters of the children had arrived. Each day began with one 10-minute, whole-class observation to observe and take notes for the CLASS and one other observational measure. Then, the observer conducted two 59-minute observation cycles that included periods to observe and take notes on the CLASS, as well the other measure.

Induction Study

(Primary Investigator: Dr. Robert Pianta, University of Virginia)

Study summary: As a part of the Teachers for a New Era project funded by the Carnegie Corporation, the University of Virginia sponsored a program to provide mentoring support to first- and second-year students in several local districts. Classroom observations were conducted as a part of this project.

Number of classrooms: 33

Location: Southeastern city

Sampling: First-year teachers in two school districts agreed to participate in the study of an induction support program.

Time of year: Fall

Observation procedure: Observations occurred in the fall and consisted of four 20-minute observation cycles, typically starting at the beginning of the school day.

NICHD Study of Early Child Care and Youth Development

(Primary Investigator: NICHD ECCRN)

Study summary: The NICHD Study of Early Child Care and Youth Development is a longitudinal prospective study of 1,364 children enrolled at birth and followed through their 15th birthdays. Information was collected on a range of family process, demographic, child care, and schooling factors as well as on a comprehensive array of developmental outcomes. Information on schooling (observations, teacher and school characteristics, school outcomes) was collected periodically while the students were in grades K–10. Observations of the study participants in their classrooms were performed in first, third, and fifth grades.

Number of classrooms: For each grade (first, third, and fifth), approximately 900 classrooms were observed.

Location: Ten sites around the country; observations were drawn from more than 1,000 school districts

Sampling: Classrooms in which the study participants were enrolled

Time of Year: Spring

Observation procedure: Observations were conducted in the spring starting at the beginning of the school day for the classrooms involved. Repeated cycles of observation were then conducted, with ratings made at the end of the 20-minute observation window, for up to four cycles for the first-grade classrooms and eight cycles for the third- and fifth-grade classrooms.

GENERAL STATISTICS

What information does the CLASS provide about classrooms?

Table A.1 presents descriptive information about the CLASS from the six studies described previously that used the CLASS. These data are not intended to be nationally representative. Data from the NCEDL studies provide information on a large number of classrooms and, for preschool in particular, were selected to get a representative sample of the geographic areas included in the study. Data from older classrooms come from small, regional studies.

Looking across data from these studies, several findings are notable. First, across all studies there is considerable variability for all dimensions except Negative Climate. Overcontrol also displayed relatively low variability and for this and other reasons, Overcontrol was revised into the new dimension Regard for Student Perspectives. Scores are adequately distributed across the 7-point scale, although Concept Development, Quality of Feedback, and Language Modeling are skewed to the lower end of the distribution.

Although the varying sampling strategies prevent making strong statements about change in CLASS scores across grades, there appears to be a trend for Concept Development and Quality of Feedback to increase with grade level. Scores on the other dimensions remain relatively constant.

These data also suggest that CLASS scores are not dramatically affected by observation procedures. The studies reported here used similar observational frameworks but implemented observations with additional measures or different numbers of intervals. Notably, however, the findings are comparable. Of particular note is that data collected for the MTP project were coded from videotape; however, scores closely parallel those from other preschool classrooms with a few exceptions. Productivity is higher, likely due to the fact that teachers tended to send in video of lessons; many failed to include transition times, which may be less productive. The slightly higher Concept Development and Quality of Feedback scores also may be a result of this process. However, even though teachers did the video-

Table A.1. Descriptive statistics (*M, SD, Range*) on CLASS® across six studies

		Preschool (MS/SWEEP)	Preschool (MTP)	Kindergarten (MS)	Third grade (4Rs)	K–5 (Induction)	Grades 1–5 (Responsive Classroom)
	N	694	164	730	82	33	88
Positive Climate	*M*	5.28	5.21	5.14	4.44	5.43	4.91
	SD	(.88)	(.90)	(.74)	(1.17)	(1.12)	(.93)
	Range	1.5–7.0	2.7–7.0	2.5–6.8	2.0–6.8	3.3–7.0	2.5–7.0
Negative Climate	*M*	1.55	1.63	1.55	2.22	1.17	1.35
	SD	(.68)	(.69)	(.65)	(1.16)	(.40)	(.65)
	Range	1.0–6.3	1.0–4.6	1–5.26	1.0–6.7	1.0–2.5	1.0–3.5
Teacher Sensitivity	*M*	4.70	4.34	4.64	4.60	5.52	4.74
	SD	(.96)	(.94)	(.86)	(1.10)	(1.00)	(1.01)
	Range	1.5–7.0	2.0–7.0	1.9–6.8	1.3–6.8	3.0–7.0	2.5–6.5
Regard for Student Perspectives	*M*		4.36		4.28	4.77	
	SD		(.97)		(1.08)	(.91)	
	Range		2.0–6.3		1.7–6.0	2.8–6.5	
Overcontrol	*M*	1.59		1.91			1.14
	SD	(.73)		(.75)			(.43)
	Range	1.0–5.6		1.0–5.4			1.0–3.0
Behavior Management	*M*	4.97	4.94	5.18	4.98	5.90	5.14
	SD	(.97)	(.88)	(.79)	(1.29)	(.95)	(.95)
	Range	1–7	2.0–6.7	1.9–7.0	1.0–7.0	4.0–7.0	3.5–7.0
Productivity	*M*	4.50	5.41	4.67	4.69	5.96	4.98
	SD	(.91)	(.82)	(.73)	(1.14)	(.79)	(1.00)
	Range	1–6.9	3.0–7.0	1.8–6.5	1.5–6.8	4.3–7.0	2.5–7.0
Instructional Learning Formats	*M*	3.90	4.57	4.11	4.21	5.22	4.23
	SD	(1.13)	(.78)	(.84)	(1.22)	(.95)	(.73)
	Range	1–7	2.0–6.33	1.1–6.1	1.0–6.5	3.3–7.0	2.5–6.0
Concept Development	*M*	2.09	2.69	2.11	3.84	4.22	3.82
	SD	(.89)	(.68)	(.74)	(1.32)	(1.07)	(1.01)
	Range	1–5.31	1.5–4.4	1–5.21	1.0–6.5	2.0–6.0	1.5–6.5
Quality of Feedback	*M*	2.04	2.87	1.84	3.54	4.61	4.77
	SD	(.96)	(.85)	(.64)	(1.31)	(1.15)	(1.03)
	Range	1–5.8	1.0–6.0	1.0–5.2	1.00–6.00	2.0–7.0	2.0–7.0
Language Modeling	*M*		2.85				
	SD		(.73)				
	Range		1.0–5.0				

Key: MS = Multi-State Study of Preschool; SWEEP = State-Wide Early Education Programs; MTP = MyTeachingPartner; *M* = Mean; *SD* = Standard Deviation.

taping themselves and mailed the tapes to the researchers, they did not appear to edit content in a way that would dramatically affect their scores. Levels of Positive Climate, Negative Climate, and Teacher Sensitivity are similar to those found in preschools across the nation. A more thorough examination of ways in which observation procedures may affect CLASS scores is reported below.

Table A.2. Correlations among CLASS® dimensions in preschool (top numbers; MS/SWEEP studies; *n* = 694) and third grade (bottom numbers; 4R study; *n* = 82) classrooms*

	1	2	3	4	5	6	7	8	9	10
1. Positive Climate	–	-.63	.79	–	-.42	.69	.69	.36	.45	.49
2. Negative Climate	-.63	–	-.58	–	.52	-.54	-.50	-.17	-.19	-.23
3. Teacher Sensitivity	.77	-.64	–	–	-.44	.64	.65	.27	.50	.41
4. Regard for Student Perspectives	.78	-.52	.75	–	–	–	–	–	–	–
5. Overcontrol	–	–	–	–	–	-.23	-.30	.08	-.11	-.16
6. Behavior Management	.51	-.70	.66	.47	–	–	.71	.32	.52	.45
7. Productivity	.38	-.53	.58	.46	–	.72		.42	.64	.50
8. Concept Development	.46	-.34	.71	.63	–	.44	.54	–	.43	.65
9. Instructional Learning Formats	.63	-.50	.70	.67	–	.55	.65	.54	–	.40
10. Quality of Feedback	.55	-.50	.79	.70	–	.57	.56	.82	.60	–
11. Student Engagement	.54	-.56	.59	.56	–	.70	.76	.36	.75	.45

Note: MS = Multi-State Study of Preschool; SWEEP = State-Wide Early Education Programs.
*All correlations above .10 are significant at *p* < .001.

How do the dimensions of the CLASS relate to one another?

As displayed in Table A.2, the CLASS dimensions are moderately to highly correlated with one another. The top numbers in this correlation matrix provide data on the association between CLASS dimensions within the Multi-State/SWEEP pre-kindergarten sample. The bottom numbers in the matrix includes data from The 4Rs Program of third-grade classrooms in New York City.

The CLASS was developed using a theoretical framework suggesting three major domains of classroom process (refer to Chapter 1 of the CLASS manual for more information). To test the degree to which data from actual classrooms matched this theoretical framework, we conducted confirmatory factor analyses on data from each of the studies mentioned previously, with the exception of the Induction study, which did not have enough classrooms. Table A.3 presents the results of these analyses. The factor loadings are in the moderate to high range, and each domain has adequate internal consistency across the studies. The Emotional Support and Instructional Support domains have higher internal consistency and more consistent factor loadings than does the Classroom Organization domain. The fit indices are not optimal. However, given the strong theoretical basis of these domains and high levels of internal consistency across domains, we recommend that users of the CLASS create CLASS domain composites accordingly.

When the classroom observations derived from the COS scales were subject to a similar set of correlational and confirmatory factor analyses (Hamre et al., 2006), the findings revealed a very similar pattern of results both in terms of bivariate associations and in terms of model fit for a three-factor model, even when identical scales were not available.

Table A.3. Confirmatory factor analysis results on CLASS® from six studies

Study	NCEDL Multi-State Pre-K	SWEEP Pre-K	MTP Pre-K	NCEDL Multi-State Kindergarten	4Rs
Emotional Support			Factor Loading*		
Positive Climate	0.91	0.91	0.92	0.93	0.91
Teacher Sensitivity	0.98	0.81	0.91	0.96	0.92
Regard for Student Perspectives			0.85		0.85
Internal consistency (alpha)	0.94	0.85	0.92	0.94	0.91
Classroom Organization			Factor Loading*		
Behavior Management	0.81	0.80	0.70	0.81	0.71
Productivity	0.92	0.87	0.56	0.84	0.56
Instructional Learning Formats	0.85	0.66	0.87	0.62	0.86
Internal consistency (alpha)	0.89	0.81	0.76	0.79	0.84
Instructional Support			Factor Loading*		
Concept Development	0.92	0.79	0.79	0.86	0.69
Quality of Feedback	0.83	0.93	0.82	0.88	0.95
Language Modeling			0.86		
Internal consistency (alpha)	0.89	0.81	0.86	0.79	0.90
Indices of fit Chi-Square (df)	85.3 (11)	56.1 (11)	84.7 (24)	157.7 (11)	66.8 (17)
RMSEA	0.17	0.10	0.13	0.14	0.14
GFI	0.91	0.97	0.89	0.94	0.90
AGFI	0.77	0.92	0.80	0.86	0.79
CFI	0.95	0.98	0.93	0.96	0.93
TLI	0.90	0.95	0.90	0.92	0.89

Notes: Values are standardized regression weights. Factor variances were constrained to 1.

*Factor loading was set to 1 so the model achieved identifiability.

Key: SWEEP = State-Wide Early Education Programs; MTP = MyTeachingPartner; RMSEA = Root Mean Square Error of Approximation; GFI = Goodness of Fit Index; AGFI = Adjusted Goodness of Fit Index; CFI = Comparative Fit Index; TLI = Tucker-Lewis Index.

RELIABILITY

How do people become reliable users of the CLASS?

Reliability refers to the degree to which an instrument is free from random error associated with the process of measuring the construct of interest. One step in minimizing random error in the CLASS involves using training materials that provide potential observers with a clear and comprehensive understanding of the instrument's purposes and procedures. As a part of the CLASS training, trainees watch multiple videotaped segments that are consensus coded by at least three master CLASS coders. The consensus ratings establish a standard by which to judge the accuracy of ratings made by trainees; ratings that are not in agreement with the consensus ratings reflect a high degree of random error that is used to pinpoint additional training needs. At the end of training, potential users take a reliability test in which they watch and code classroom segments. On these reliability tests, we have achieved an average interrater reliability (within one point of

Table A.4. Interrater agreement (within 1) on CLASS® dimensions

Item	% within 1
Positive Climate	84.8
Negative Climate	93.9
Teacher Sensitivity	81.8
Regard for Student Perspectives	78.8
Behavior Management	93.9
Productivity	96.9
Instructional Learning Formats	78.8
Concept Development	84.8
Quality of Feedback	84.8
Language Modeling	84.8
All Items	87.1

master codes) of 87 percent. The same procedures were followed for the NICHD SEC-CYD observations using the COS.

How much consistency is there across users of the CLASS?

To assess interrater reliability of the CLASS items, 30-minute digital videotapes that were submitted by teachers participating in the MTP study were viewed independently by two observers. Double-coding procedures were conducted at two times during the first year of data collection, and two observers coded a total of 33 tapes. Ratings that were within 1 point of each other (along the 1–7 rating scale) were considered to reflect an acceptable degree of accuracy in ratings. For each item, the percentage of tapes that had scores within 1 point of each other is presented in Table A.4. Similar levels of reliability have been obtained in live observations.

The information from reliability analyses for the large number of observers used for the NICHD SECCYD observations are available on the project web site and in published reports (e.g., NICHD ECCRN, 2002, 2005a, 2006b) and indicate nearly identical levels of agreement as those reported previously for the CLASS.

How stable are scores on the CLASS?

Across Cycles

Many users of the CLASS are interested in minimizing the number of observation cycles in order to reduce cost. The data presented next suggest that CLASS scores are highly stable across time and that observations for the recommended four cycles (about 2 hours) provide an adequate sampling of classroom quality across the three CLASS domains. Stability across cycles was assessed in preschool and third-grade classrooms using data from

Table A.5. Correlations between cycle and total score for CLASS® dimensions and domains in preschool (PS; *n* = 240) and third grade (*n* = 68)

	Cycle 1 with Cycles 1–4		Cycles 1 and 2 with Cycles 1–4		Cycles 1–3 with Cycles 1–4		Cycles 1–4 with Spring Score
	Preschool	Third	Preschool	Third	Preschool	Third	Preschool
Positive Climate	.85	.87	.93	.93	.98	.98	.90
Negative Climate	.77	.83	.92	.92	.97	.97	.89
Teacher Sensitivity	.86	.82	.94	.93	.98	.98	.90
Overcontrol/Regard for Student Perspectives	.81	.78	.89	.92	.96	.97	.90
Behavior Management	.85	.80	.93	.95	.98	.98	.89
Productivity	.80	.68	.90	.87	.97	.96	.84
Instructional Learning Formats	.79	.78	.90	.91	.96	.97	.87
Concept Development	.81	.74	.91	.91	.98	.97	.91
Quality of Feedback	.79	.72	.90	.91	.97	.98	.88
Emotional Support	.87	.88	.95	.95	.98	.98	.91
Classroom Organization	.82	.78	.92	.94	.98	.98	.91
Instructional Support	.84	.74	.92	.92	.97	.98	.89

the NCEDL Multi-State Study of Prekindergarten and The 4Rs Program of third-grade classrooms in New York City. Table A.5 provides correlations between the score a classroom received in the first; first and second; and first, second, and third cycles and the total score, which was the sum of scores across the first four cycles. As expected, correlations between earlier cycles and the total score go up as more cycles are included because these scores are a part of the total score. It is important to note, however, that correlations between the first cycle with the total score are moderate to high, ranging from .68 for Productivity in third grade to .87 for Positive Climate in third grade. By completing two cycles, correlations with the final score are uniformly high with almost all correlations above .90 in both preschool and third-grade classrooms.

Finally, for the preschool sample, we examined the degree to which the first four cycles correlated with the final score, which was obtained over 2–3 days from an average of 15.7 cycles (*SD* = 5.3; *Range* = 8–32). Results suggest that four cycles provide a representative sampling of classrooms, with correlations ranging from .84 for Productivity to .91 for Concept Development.

Table A.6 provides another way of examining stability by assessing the degree of internal consistency of CLASS scores across two, three, and four cycles. Mirroring the previously mentioned results, these results suggest a high degree of internal consistency for the CLASS scores across cycles. Internal consistency is somewhat higher among the Emotional Support dimensions than among the Classroom Organization or Instructional Support dimensions.

Table A.6. Internal consistencies for CLASS® dimensions and domains for 2, 3, and 4 cycles in preschool (*n* = 240) and third grade (*n* = 68)

	Alpha across 4 cycles		Alpha across 3 cycles		Alpha across 2 cycles	
	Preschool	Third	Preschool	Third	Preschool	Third
Positive Climate	.89	.87	.86	.88	.81	.87
Negative Climate	.86	.83	.82	.84	.69	.84
Teacher Sensitivity	.90	.85	.87	.83	.83	.79
Overcontrol/ Regard for Student Perspectives	.80	.80	.79	.80	.78	.73
Behavior Management	.89	.87	.87	.85	.85	.77
Productivity	.82	.76	.80	.71	.74	.71
Instructional Learning Formats	.79	.82	.80	.79	.76	.77
Concept Development	.83	.81	.79	.74	.76	.63
Quality of Feedback	.84	.83	.81	.76	.77	.75
Emotional Support	.91	.89	.89	.90	.85	.88
Classroom Organization	.87	.86	.86	.84	.83	.80
Instructional Support	.86	.84	.83	.78	.79	.73

One final way of examining stability concerns the degree to which there may be systematic *mean* changes in CLASS scores across the school day. Table A.7 presents the mean and standard deviations on CLASS scores across the first four cycles from the Multi-State Prekindergarten and The 4Rs third-grade samples. Repeated measures analyses were conducted to examine the extent to which the quality of the three domains were associated with the observation cycle. Within preschool classrooms across four consecutive observation cycles within a day, the cycle was not associated with observations of Instructional Support. Quality of Emotional Support had a significant association across four cycles, $F(3,239) = 41.4$, $p = .000$, such that emotional support decreased across observation cycles in a linear fashion. Cycle did not have a significant linear association with the quality of Classroom Organization; however, there was a significant quadratic relation between cycle and quality of the organizational context $F(3,239) = 4.40$, $p = .037$.

In the third-grade sample, there was not a significant effect of time on either the Emotional Support or Instructional Support domains, $F(3, 68) = .12$, $p = .73$ and $F(3, 68) = 1.36$, $p = .25$, respectively. There was a significant linear trend from classroom organization, $F(3, 68) = 8.29$, $p < .01$, with quality decreasing over the course of the four cycles.

These cross-cycle, within-day patterns are nearly identical for the morning-long and day-long observations conducted in the NICHD SECCYD using the COS.

Across Days in Week

Another question of concern to those conducting classroom observations is the extent to which one day is representative of general classroom practices. Within the NCEDL MS data, preschool classrooms were observed on 2, typically consecutive, days during the

Table A.7. Mean and standard deviation of CLASS® dimensions and domains for each of four cycles in preschool and third-grade classrooms

		Preschool[1] (n = 240)				Third Grade[2] (n = 68)			
		Cycle 1	Cycle 2	Cycle 3	Cycle 4	Cycle 1	Cycle 2	Cycle 3	Cycle 4
Positive Climate	M	5.38	5.25	5.21	4.99	4.35	4.53	4.46	4.58
	SD	(1.08)	(1.06)	(1.09)	(1.20)	(1.56)	(1.32)	(1.35)	(1.21)
Negative Climate	M	1.40	1.58	1.69	1.81	2.18	2.17	2.31	2.25
	SD	(0.74)	(0.89)	(0.94)	(1.16)	(1.39)	(1.31)	(1.26)	(1.22)
Teacher Sensitivity	M	4.94	4.69	4.64	4.35	4.73	4.68	4.58	4.59
	SD	(1.20)	(1.31)	(1.37)	(1.38)	(1.35)	(1.23)	(1.26)	(1.24)
Overcontrol[1]/ Regard for Student Perspectives[2]	M	1.89	1.94	1.90	1.85	4.23	4.26	4.54	4.41
	SD	(1.19)	(1.23)	(1.22)	(1.25)	(1.38)	(1.27)	(1.28)	(1.25)
Behavior Management	M	5.25	5.08	4.93	4.75	5.28	5.06	4.97	4.76
	SD	(1.20)	(1.26)	(1.30)	(1.37)	(1.38)	(1.43)	(1.30)	(1.44)
Productivity	M	4.65	4.70	4.72	4.51	5.01	4.79	4.89	4.56
	SD	(1.38)	(1.39)	(1.31)	(1.40)	(1.31)	(1.29)	(1.36)	(1.41)
Instructional Learning Formats	M	4.03	4.33	4.61	4.41	4.30	4.31	4.54	4.10
	SD	(1.43)	(1.43)	(1.30)	(1.36)	(1.53)	(1.37)	(1.34)	(1.43)
Concept Development	M	2.41	2.41	2.46	2.24	3.97	3.87	4.31	3.85
	SD	(1.46)	(1.53)	(1.49)	(1.42)	(1.57)	(1.58)	(1.62)	(1.73)
Quality of Feedback	M	1.90	1.83	1.87	1.84	3.65	3.56	3.72	3.62
	SD	(1.08)	(1.06)	(1.10)	(1.09)	(1.56)	(1.55)	(1.68)	(1.54)
Emotional Support	M	5.76	5.61	5.56	5.42	4.78	4.83	4.82	4.83
	SD	(0.81)	(0.87)	(0.88)	(0.99)	(1.22)	(1.01)	(1.00)	(1.00)
Classroom Organization	M	4.64	4.70	4.75	4.56	4.86	4.72	4.80	4.46
	SD	(1.09)	(1.13)	(1.09)	(1.16)	(1.15)	(1.09)	(1.06)	(1.18)
Instructional Support	M	2.15	2.12	2.17	2.04	3.80	3.72	4.01	3.73
	SD	(1.13)	(1.18)	(1.15)	(1.11)	(1.47)	(1.46)	(1.53)	(1.52)

spring. Results presented in Table A.8 suggest a high degree of stability, with correlations between the 2 days ranging from .73 for Productivity to .85 for Teacher Sensitivity. There were small but significant mean changes across several of the dimensions, with a general trend toward lower-quality scores on the second day. Given that there is no reason to expect a systematic difference in quality across 2 consecutive days, these small changes may be due to observer bias in which scores become slightly lower over time. Again, however, although these differences are statistically significant, they are relatively small effects; correlations between the 2 days are high.

Across the School Year

As presented in Table A.9, scores on the CLASS also are relatively stable from fall to spring, at least across a large number of preschool programs. There are only small

Table A.8. Consistency in CLASS® means across observation days/NCEDL data (*n* = 240)

	Day 1	Day 2	Correlations between Day 1 and Day 2	Paired samples *t*-test
Positive Climate	5.11 (0.96)	5.02 (0.97)	0.83	2.29*
Negative Climate	1.68 (0.83)	1.71 (0.82)	0.78	−0.64
Teacher Sensitivity	4.52 (1.13)	4.46 (1.09)	0.85	1.70
Overcontrol/Regard for Student Perspectives	1.90 (0.95)	1.87 (0.92)	0.80	0.87
Behavior Management	4.88 (1.08)	4.76 (1.03)	0.83	3.05**
Productivity	4.45 (1.07)	4.33 (1.10)	0.73	2.35*
Instructional Learning Formats	4.17 (1.04)	4.12 (1.03)	0.79	1.11
Concept Development	2.24 (1.13)	2.13 (1.11)	0.84	2.83**
Quality of Feedback	1.75 (0.79)	1.70 (0.85)	0.82	1.57
Emotional Support	5.51 (0.79)	5.48 (0.76)	0.85	1.29
Classroom Organization	4.50 (0.93)	4.40 (0.90)	0.81	2.64**
Instructional Support	2.00 (0.88)	1.91 (0.91)	0.86	2.73**

*p < .05; **p < .01

Table A.9. Means and stability of fall and spring CLASS® scores in preschool classrooms (*n* = 240)

	Fall	Spring	Correlations between fall and spring	Paired samples *t*-test
Positive Climate	5.07	5.06	.58	0.52
Negative Climate	1.81	1.71	.38	1.57
Teacher Sensitivity	4.46	4.47	.51	−0.02
Overcontrol	2.39	1.89	.29	6.39**
Behavior Management	4.76	4.78	.64	−0.27
Productivity	4.38	4.39	.46	−0.11
Instructional Learning Formats	4.09	4.12	.53	−0.80
Concept Development	2.88	2.16	.36	8.57**
Quality of Feedback	2.06	1.71	.25	4.40**

*p < .05; **p < .01

changes in mean scores, and correlations between fall and spring range from .64 for Behavior Management to .25 for Quality of Feedback. In general, there appears to be lower levels of stability in the Instructional Support dimension than in other dimensions, with Concept Development and Quality of Feedback decreasing from fall to spring.

Data from the MTP sample allow us to examine changes over the course of the school year. Figures A.2–A.4 graph the average quality observed in classrooms across the school

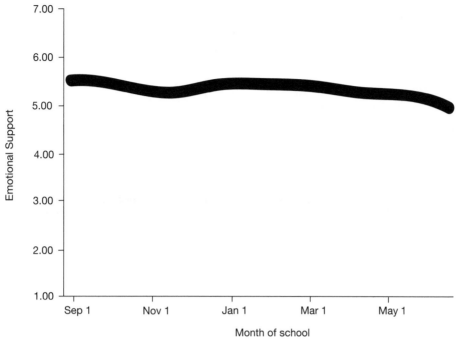

Figure A.2. Average Emotional Support in preschool classrooms across the school year.

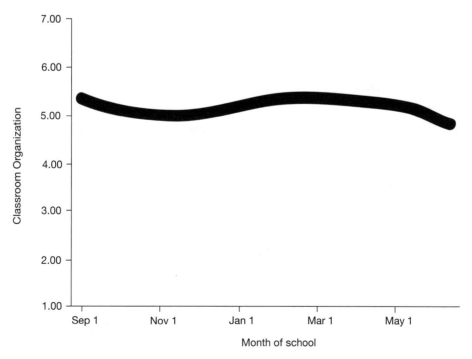

Figure A.3. Average Classroom Organization in preschool classrooms across the school year.

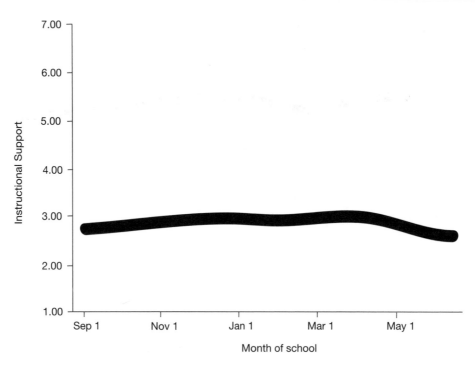

Figure A.4. Average Instructional Support in preschool classrooms across the school year.

year. These data were derived from tapes that teachers sent in every other week. The Y axis represents the average score observed across all tapes received on a given day. These are descriptive data only and should not be generalized to other grades. However, they do suggest that the CLASS may be sensitive to the fluctuations in quality that often are described around the holidays and toward the end of the school year.

Across Children and/or Days

In the NICHD SECCYD, many of these same issues were examined based on data from 4–8 observation cycles. As noted previously, these results are reported elsewhere (NICHD ECCRN, 2002, 2005) and are highly concordant with these observations using the CLASS; there is a very high degree of cross-cycle stability in 7-point rating scales of classrooms/ teachers and roughly four 20-minute observational cycles yield highly stable estimates of teacher behavior and the classroom environment.

Importantly, in the NICHD study, in more than 200 cases, the same classroom/teacher was observed on more than one occasion with a *different* child being the target of the observation. These repeated observations of the same classroom occurred because more than one child enrolled in the study happened to be assigned to that teacher. A different observer was always assigned in these circumstances. The cross-time stability of the COS rating scales for these doubly-rated classrooms was estimated using zero-order correlations for repeated scales, and these correlations all exceeded .65. These analyses indicate that 7-point ratings of the classroom setting and teacher behavior are highly stable and are not dependent on occasion or even the child who may be the target or reason for observing that classroom.

VALIDITY

Does the CLASS measure constructs of importance in classrooms (face and construct validity)?

The CLASS was developed based on an extensive literature review on classroom practices shown to relate to students' social and academic development in schools. The dimensions were derived from a review of constructs assessed in classroom observation instruments used in child care and elementary school research, literature on effective teaching practices, focus groups, and extensive piloting. Throughout this process, numerous experts in classroom quality and teaching effectiveness have agreed that the CLASS measures aspects of the classroom that are of importance in determining student performance, suggesting considerable face validity.

How does the CLASS relate to other measures of classroom quality and associated constructs (criterion validity)?

Criterion validity assesses the extent to which a measure is associated empirically with other measures of similar constructs. Table A.10 presents the results from analyses examining relationships between the CLASS (Pre-K version) and various other measures of classrooms and teachers (Pianta et al., 2005). Classrooms with higher Emotional Support, Classroom Organization, and Instructional Support received higher scores on two factors of the Early Childhood Environment Rating Scale, Revised Edition (ECERS–R), the most commonly used measure of quality in early childhood classrooms. The first ECERS–R factor, Interactions, describes the extent to which classrooms promote teacher–child interactions,

Table A.10. Correlations between CLASS® Pre-K and ECERS–R, Snapshot, teacher depression, and adult-centered attitudes

CLASS domain	ECERS–R		Snapshot			
	Interactions	Provisions	% time in literacy and language	% time in math	% time in adult-elaborated interactions	% time not engaged
Emotional Support	.63**	.33**	.22**	.13*	.43**	−.35**
Classroom Organization	.55**	.35**	.17**	.14**	.29**	−.42**
Instructional Support	.45**	.36*	.12*	.03	.23**	−.32**

*p < .01; **p < .000

encourage children to communicate and use language, and provide effective discipline; the second factor, Provisions, assesses the availability of furnishings and materials. Consistent with the CLASS focus on classroom interactions, it is not surprising that the CLASS had stronger associations with the Interactions factor.

The Emerging Academics Snapshot (Ritchie, Howes, Kraft-Sayre, & Weiser, 2001) is a time-sampling method used to assess the percentage of time spent on various activities. Within the MS Study of state-funded pre-k programs, classrooms with higher CLASS scores spent more time on literacy and language and math activities. The somewhat lower correlations between the CLASS Instructional Support domain and time spent in literacy and math is not surprising given that this domain focuses on quality, not quantity, of instruction. Children in classrooms with higher CLASS scores spent more time in elaborated interactions with adults and significantly more time engaged.

How does the CLASS relate to students' academic and social development (predictive validity)?

The CLASS was designed to assess classroom-level processes that are directly associated with children's performance. Results from the NCEDL Multi-State Study provide evidence that classroom quality, as assessed by the CLASS, is associated with children's performance at the end of preschool as well as gains in their performance across the preschool year (Howes et al., in press; Mashburn et al., in press). In this study, the association between the CLASS and children's outcomes was assessed after adjusting for a variety of covariates, including maternal education, ethnicity, and gender. The ECERS–R scales also were included in these analyses. The most consistent and robust classroom quality dimension for predicting growth across time was the Instructional Support of the classroom as assessed by the CLASS. In classrooms in which the teacher promoted higher-order thinking and creativity and gave verbal feedback relevant to performance, children's receptive and expressive language, understanding of prereading concepts, and applied mathematics skills all increased. The CLASS Emotional Support domain was associated with growth in children's expressive and receptive language scores as well as decreases in teacher-reported behavior problems (Howes et al., in press; Mashburn et al., in press).

In the NICHD SECCYD, which used the COS as the method for observing classrooms in first, third, and fifth grades, a number of published reports have presented results pertaining to the predictive validity of global rating scales very similar to those in the CLASS, and so those results are relevant for the present discussion. It is important to note that nearly all of the analyses related to classroom effects either use growth curves and predict change in children's functioning and/or adjust for a host of family and demographic factors known to predict the child outcomes under consideration (e.g., achievement tests, ratings of social adjustment). The findings from the NICHD SECCYD indicate significant increments in explained variance in achievement and social outcomes for observed classroom features of emotional and instructional quality derived from the COS ratings (NICHD, 2003, 2005b, 2006a). A recent study using the NICHD data indicated these observed features of the classroom environment to be particularly important for closing achievement gaps for at-risk children in first grade (Hamre & Pianta, 2005).

SUMMARY

Ratings from the CLASS provide important descriptive information about the current status of early childhood and elementary classrooms and also have a predictive value in academic and social outcomes for children. As such, the CLASS can be a useful tool for researchers, administrators, and policymakers wanting a standardized measure of classroom processes that are empirically linked to important student outcomes. See the Technical Manual at http://www.classobservation.com for updates.

REFERENCES

Bogard, K., & Takanishi, R. (2005). PK-3: An aligned and coordinated approach to education for children 3 to 8 years old. *Social Policy Report: A Publication of the Society for Research in Child Development, 19*(3), 1–24.

Early, D., Barbarin, O., Bryant, D., Burchinal, M., Chang, F., Clifford, R., et al. (2005). *Prekindergarten in eleven states: NCEDL's Multi-State Study of Prekindergarten and Study of State-Wide Early Education Programs.* Retrieved December 1, 2005, from http://www.fpg.unc.edu/NCEDL/pdfs/ SWEEP _MS_summary_final.pdf

Greenberg, M.T., Domitrovich, C., & Bumbarger, B. (2001). The prevention of mental disorders in school-aged children: Current state of the field. *Prevention and Treatment, 4.*

Hamre, B.K., Mashburn, A., Pianta, R.C., & Downer, J. (2006). *Validation of 3-factor model for classroom quality across preschool to fifth grade.* Manuscript submitted for publication.

Hamre, B.K., & Pianta, R.C. (2005). Can instructional and emotional support in the first grade classroom make a difference for children at risk of school failure? *Child Development, 76*(5), 949–967.

Howes, C., Burchinal, M., Pianta, R.C., Bryant, D., Early, D., Clifford, R., et al. (in press). Ready to learn? Children's pre-academic achievement in pre-kindergarten programs. *Developmental Psychology.*

Mashburn, A.J., Pianta, R.C., Hamre, B.K., Downer, J.T., Barbarin, O., Bryant, D., Burchinal, M., et al. (in press). Pre-k program standards and children's development of academic and language skills. *Child Development.*

Morrison, F.J., & Connor, C.M. (2002). Understanding schooling effects on early literacy: A working research strategy. *Journal of School Psychology, 40*(6), 493–500.

NICHD Early Child Care Research Network. (2002). The relation of global first grade classroom environment to structural classroom features, teacher, and student behaviors. *Elementary School Journal, 102*(5), 367–387.

NICHD Early Child Care Research Network. (2003). Social functioning in first grade: Prediction from home, child care and concurrent school experience. *Child Development, 74,* 1639–1662.

NICHD Early Child Care Research Network. (2005a). A day in third grade: A large-scale study of classroom quality and teacher and student behavior. *The Elementary School Journal, 105,* 305–323.

NICHD Early Child Care Research Network. (2005b). Predicting individual differences in attention, memory, and planning in first graders from experiences at home, child care, and school. *Developmental Psychology, 41,* 99–114.

NICHD Early Child Care Research Network. (2006a). *Classroom quality and trajectories of academic achievement in elementary school.* Manuscript in preparation.

NICHD Early Child Care Research Network. (2006b). *Observations in 5th grade classrooms and stability of classroom experiences from 1st and 3rd grade.* Manuscript in preparation.

Pianta, R.C. (2006). Teacher–child relationships and early literacy. In D. Dickinson & S. Newman (Eds.), *Handbook of early literacy research,* (Vol. 2, pp. 149–162). New York: The Guilford Press.

Pianta, R.C., Howes, C., Burchinal, M., Bryant, D., Clifford, R., Early, C., et al. (2005). Features of pre-kindergarten programs, classrooms, and teachers: Do they predict observed classroom quality and child–teacher interactions? *Applied Developmental Science, 9*(3), 144–159.

Pianta, R.C., Mashburn, A.J., Downer, J.T., Hamre, B.K., & Justice, L. (2007). *Effects of web-mediated professional development resources on teacher–child interactions in pre-kindergarten classrooms.* Manuscript submitted for publication.

Ritchie, S., Howes, C., Kraft-Sayre, M., & Weiser, B. (2001). *Emerging Academic Snapshot.* Unpublished.

Rutter, M., & Maughan, B. (2002). School effectiveness findings, 1979–2002. *Journal of School Psychology, 40*(6), 451–475.

Index

Tables and figures are indicated by *t* and *f,* respectively.

Your quick-guide to  products

Schools across the country trust the CLASS® observational tool—the most accurate, efficient way to assess the quality of interactions between children and teachers. With versions for Infant, Toddler, Pre-K, and K–3 classrooms, the CLASS® tool

- **Is both valid and reliable**, proven through research and testing in diverse early childhood settings
- **Highlights areas of strength and areas for growth**—ideal for guiding improvement efforts
- **Addresses your program's most urgent needs**, including accountability efforts, professional development, program planning, and research

NEW! CLASS® Infant

Developed for use with children from birth to 18 months, the NEW CLASS® Infant tool assesses 4 dimensions of teacher–child interaction: relational climate, teacher sensitivity, facilitated exploration, and early language support.

Manual—US$54.95
Stock #: BA-76047
2014
ISBN 978-1-59757-604-7

Forms—US$30.00
Stock #: BA-76054
2014
ISBN 978-1-59857-605-4
Package of 10

CLASS® Toddler

For use with children from 15–36 months, the toddler version covers two domains of teacher-child interaction: Emotional and Behavior Support (5 dimensions) and Engaged Support for Learning (3 dimensions).

Toddler Manual—US$54.95
Stock #: BA-72599
2012
ISBN 978-1-59857-259-9

Toddler Forms—US$30.00
Stock #: BA-72605
2012
ISBN 978-1-59857-260-5
Package of 10

CLASS® Observation Training is an essential prerequisite for accurate use of the CLASS® tool.
Learn more about it at www.teachstone.com/training-programs.

Easy to order! | Call 1-800-638-3775 or visit www.brookespublishing.com | **BA is your list code.**

CLASS® Pre-K, CLASS® K–3

Both CLASS® Pre-K and CLASS® K–3 focus on three key domains of teacher–student interaction—Emotional Support, Classroom Organization, and Instructional Support that matter for young children's growth and development. And now Spanish-speaking CLASS® observers can use the Spanish CLASS® Manual and Forms, Pre-K as they observe early childhood classrooms.

Manuals

Pre-K English—US$54.95
Stock #: BA-69414
2008
ISBN 978-1-55766-941-4

Pre-K Spanish—US$54.95
Stock #: BA-72384
2012
ISBN 978-1-59857-238-4

K–3—US$54.95
Stock #: BA-69421
2008
ISBN 978-1-55766-942-1

Forms

Pre-K–3 English—US$30.00
Stock #: BA-69438
2008
ISBN 978-1-55766-943-8
Package of 10

Pre-K Spanish—US$30.00
Stock #: BA-72360
2012
ISBN 978-1-59857-236-0
Package of 10

CLASS® Dimensions Overview

Available in convenient packages of 5, this tri-fold laminated sheet shows evaluators an at-a-glance overview of the CLASS® dimensions.

Each Dimensions Overview—US$30.00 • 6 pages, tri-fold • package of 5

Infant
Stock #: BA-76061
2014
ISBN 978-1-59857-606-1

Toddler
Stock #: BA-72612
2012
ISBN 978-1-59857-261-2

Pre-K–3 English
Stock #: BA-70885
2009
ISBN 978-1-59857-088-5

Pre-K Spanish
Stock #: BA-72353
2012
ISBN 978-1-59857-235-3

CLASS® Dimensions Guide

Introduce teachers to the dimensions of the CLASS® tool with these concise guides, each with practical teaching tips. A great way to get teachers on board with the CLASS® observation!

Each guide—US$19.95 • 2011 • 28 pages • 8 ½ x 11 • saddle-stitched

Infant English
Stock #: BA-78119
ISBN 978-1-59857-811-9

Infant Spanish
Stock #: BA-79666
ISBN 978-1-59857-966-6

K–3(English only)
Stock #: BA-72308
ISBN 978-1-59857-230-8

Toddler English
Stock #: BA-72292
ISBN 978-1-59857-229-2

Toddler Spanish
Stock #: BA-76078
ISBN 978-1-59857-607-8

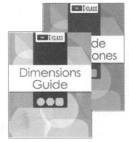

Pre-K English
Stock #: BA-72278
ISBN 978-1-59857-227-8

Pre-K Spanish
Stock #: BA-72285
ISBN 978-1-59857-228-5